Body Defining

Drop Pounds,
Firm Flab
& Maximize
Lean Muscle Lines
in Just Six
Short Weeks

Ellington Darden, Ph.D.

CB
CONTEMPORARY BOOKS

Library of Congress Cataloging-in-Publication Data

Darden, Ellington, 1943–
    Body Defining / Ellington Darden.
        p.   cm.
    ISBN 0-8092-3232-4
    1. Reducing exercises.   2. Physical fitness for women.   I. Title.
RA781.6.D368   1996
613.7—dc20   95-41470
                                                              CIP

Front cover photo by Timothy Tew

Interior photos by Ellington Darden (pp. 13, 17, 23, 111, 119, and 126), Ken Hutchins (pp. 7, 26, and 108), Chris Lund (pp. 2 and 27), Alicia Tannery (p. 6) and Timothy Tew (pp. x, 30, 32, 58, 60, 94, 96, and 132)

Exercise drawings (Chapters 14, 16, and 18) by Shum Rojas

Interior design by Frank Loose Design

Published by Contemporary Books
A division of NTC/Contemporary Publishing Group, Inc.
4255 West Touhy Avenue, Lincolnwood (Chicago), Illinois 60712-1975 U.S.A.
Printed in the United States of America
International Standard Book Number: 0-8092-3232-4
00 01 02 03 04 05 QB 22 21 20 19 18 17 16 15 14 13 12 11 10 9 8 7 6 5

Other books of interest by Ellington Darden

Two Weeks to a Tighter Tummy
The Nautilus Book
The Nautilus Diet
The Nautilus Bodybuilding Book
High-Intensity Strength Training
The Six-Week Fat-to-Muscle Makeover
Nutrition for Athletes
High-Intensity Home Training
The Complete Encyclopedia of Weight Loss, Body Shaping, and Slenderizing
The Athlete's Guide to Sports Medicine
How to Lose Body Fat
Soft Steps to a Hard Body
Living Longer Stronger

Make a commitment
to get
great results!

Contents

Acknowledgments

Sincere thanks go to the following people who helped in the preparation of *Body Defining:*

Kara Leverte edited the manuscript and offered a number of valuable suggestions.

Timothy Tew took the full-page photographs throughout the book and the photo on the front cover.

Shum Rojas created the exercise illustrations from photographs by Boyd Welsch.

Lisa Danver, Tami Sullivan, Elena Welsch, Amy Knuckles, Jill McCann, Brenda Smedley, and Georgina Fieldus demonstrated the recommended exercises.

Rachelle Richardson input the manuscript into her word processor and made the necessary revisions. Rachelle also modeled for the front cover and for other pictures in the book.

Pam Ferrell of Athletic Lady in Gainesville, Florida, supplied Rachelle's exercise apparel.

Special appreciation goes to Joe Cirulli and the Gainesville Health & Fitness Center and to all the women who participated in the research for this book.

Warning

The programs in this book are intended only for healthy women. Women with health problems should not follow these programs without a physician's approval. Before beginning any exercise or dietary routine, always consult your doctor.

The *Body Defining* Concept

Body defining means delineating the muscles of your calves, thighs, hips, midsection, shoulders, and arms—and making them visible through your skin.

A defined look requires a minimum of fat, combined with selective muscular development. Eating, hydrating, exercising, and resting—in precise amounts—are necessary to produce this look. But such an appearance still needs symmetry. Understanding the body's natural lines can help you accentuate height, width, and leanness.

Body Defining is a self-help course for creating a firm, strong, striking figure. The emphasis is on sharpness, as opposed to smoothness. Special attention goes to the hips and thighs, since they are the major concerns of most women.

When you've completed this course, you'll be able to see the indentations and curves of your major muscles, as well as the subtle separations between your body parts. You'll experience muscular refinement from top to bottom, from tip to toe. Your body will be well defined.

Volume comparisons of 5 pounds of fat (left) and 5 pounds of muscle reveal that fat takes up approximately 20 percent more space than muscle.

Part I

Problems, Facts, and Solutions

The one-legged calf raise is a great exercise to build, shape, and define your calves.

Chapter 1

The Number-One Fitness Problem

What is the average woman's number-one fitness problem? The answer may surprise you. It's the loss of muscle mass.

Muscle mass! I know what you're thinking:

"I don't want large muscles."

"I don't want to look like those women bodybuilders I've seen on television."

"I actually want smaller muscles."

Bear with me as I explain why larger muscles are the key to attaining the body you've always desired.

Losing as little as one-half pound of muscle can result in a gain of fat. Why? Because muscle is active tissue and makes high calorie demands, even at rest. Less muscle means a lower metabolic rate. Several studies reveal that the average woman experiences a slight decline in her metabolic rate every year, which exactly parallels her loss of muscle.

The relationship is clear: as muscle mass decreases, metabolism slows. As the average woman gets older—even if she continues to eat the same approximate number of calories per day—she gets fatter and fatter. A cycle is gradually established. Loss of muscle equals a decline in metabolic rate. This, combined with normal eating habits and the passage of time, leads to an overfat, out-of-shape body.

Muscle and Fat Changes

Since 1985, I've collected body-composition measurements on more than one thousand women of all ages. The chart below is representative of what happens to the average woman's body as she gets older.

The average woman is at her muscular peak at age 14: height, 5 feet 4 inches; body weight, 120 pounds; total muscle tissue weight, 48 pounds; fat tissue weight, 20 pounds. Her muscle-to-fat ratio is 48:20 or 2.4:1. In other words, she has 2.4 pounds of muscle for each pound of fat. Because of this high ratio of muscle to fat, her body is lean, firm, and well defined. With each successive year, however, she loses 0.5 pound of muscle and gains 1.5 pounds of fat.

The average 50-year-old woman weighs 156 pounds, which is a gain of 36 pounds of body weight since age 14. More specifically, her muscle has decreased by 18 pounds and her fat has increased by 54 pounds. Her muscle-to-fat ratio has changed from 2.4:1 to 1:2.4, which is an exact re-

MUSCLE-FAT RATIO CHANGES IN AN AVERAGE WOMAN AS SHE AGES

Age	14	20	30	40	50
Body Weight (lbs.)	120	126	136	146	156
Muscle (lbs.)	48	45	40	35	30
Fat (lbs.)	20	29	44	59	74
Percent Body Fat	16.7	23.0	32.4	40.4	47.4

versal. Furthermore, her percentage of body fat has gone from 16.7 to 47.4—a 284 percent increase.

What brings on this whopping increase in body fat? It all begins with the gradual loss of muscle mass. Of course there are other factors, such as too many dietary calories, faulty eating habits, pregnancy, hormone changes, overstress, and the natural aging process, but the shrinking of muscles remains the primary problem.

What causes the loss of muscle mass? Very simply, the answer is lack of proper exercise. Proper exercise can rebuild, reshape, and continually increase the size of your muscles.

Proper Exercise Explained

What is proper exercise? Proper exercise is movement against a resistance that can be made heavier and heavier. Such exercise has been called weightlifting, weight training, pumping iron, and strength training. I prefer the latter term—*strength training*—and it will be used throughout this book. Strength training usually refers to the use of barbells, dumbbells, and various machines that have movement arms and self-contained weight stacks. The strength-training guidelines used in *Body Defining* are based on scientific studies and practical experience that I've gotten from training more than six thousand women over the past 30 years.

Hip-and-Thigh Heavy

What I've learned allows me to design the *Body Defining* strength-training program to address specific figure problems. For example, the most prevalent figure question that women have is how to get rid of the disproportionate amount of fat around their hips and thighs. Most women, when compared with men, do have a preponderance of fat cells around their hips and thighs. Part of this large number of fat cells is attributable to hormones, pregnancy, and childbirth. The other part is connected to the loss

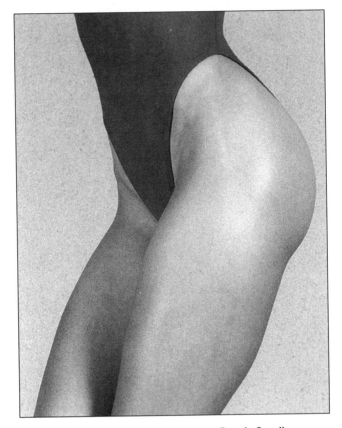

These contoured hips and thighs belong to Brenda Smedley.
Brenda went through the six-week program and built 5.13 pounds
of muscle and reduced her body fat to 14.6 percent. Remember, a
well-defined figure requires a minimum of subcutaneous fat com-
bined with strong underlying muscles.

of muscle mass. Since the largest muscles of a woman's body are located in the hips and thighs, it makes sense that most of her muscle loss would come from those areas. It also rings true that her thickest layers of fat cells—those surrounding the hips and thighs—are made even thicker and flabbier with the gradual loss of muscle and the gradual gain of fat.

This book presents a state-of-the-art strength-training program that focuses on the hips and thighs. It also includes a scientific eating plan to shrink your fat cells. You'll have a choice of strength training with machines, which are usually found in a fitness center, or dumbbells, which can be used in the privacy of your home. The eating plan is composed of foods that are available at your local supermarket. Everything about this diet has been streamlined for today's active woman.

As you lose fat and build muscle, you'll also practice actions that will produce subtle separations and indentations on your physique. In essence, your contours will become more defined.

Success Stories

The entire *Body Defining* program has been tested, evaluated, improved, and retested on thousands of women—women just like you.

Success stories of some of these women—including before-and-after photographs—appear throughout this book. Although each woman has

SUCCESS STORY: MADELINE WILDMAN, AGE 28, HEIGHT 5'10"

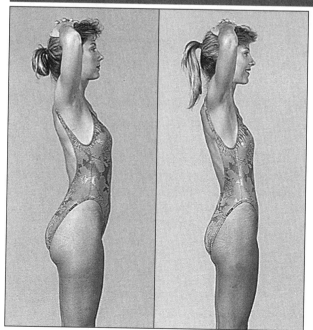

• Lost 18¼ pounds of fat

• Built 4½ pounds of muscle

• Trimmed 6 inches off her thighs in 6 weeks

"I worked harder at this program than I've ever done in my life, and I got results I never dreamed possible. I now realize that larger, stronger muscles are my best ally against the aging process."

unique physical characteristics, her body also resembles other female bodies in some respects. It will be useful for you to examine these photographs with an eye for figure shapes similar to your own. Doing so will help you come to a realistic view of what you can achieve.

Excessively Large Muscles and Genetics

You will note that none of the women pictured in this book has excessively large muscles, or looks like a bodybuilder. But several of them have large muscles and want them to be even larger. Several of the women would like to compete in bodybuilding contests.

Having excessively large muscles, however, requires rare inherited characteristics. Such a woman would have to have unusually long muscle bellies and short tendons. This combination is rare even among men. Only one person in a million inherits these traits. Furthermore, to be a successful bodybuilder—besides having excessively large muscles—a woman must be very lean. Once again, this necessitates favorable genetics, in that a person would have to have a well-below-average number of fat cells.

In spite of these seldom-seen genetic traits, many women still worry about overdeveloping their muscles. However, larger muscles are in fact the very thing they need. Adding muscle will help women to:

- melt fat away

- tighten flabby body parts

- smooth dimpled backsides

- eat more calories of favorite foods

Don't be afraid of building excessively large muscles. It won't happen. If you ever did develop a muscle that was too large, all you'd have to do is stop exercising it. Within a week, the muscle would begin to atrophy, or lose size from disuse. Remember, as I stated at the beginning of this chapter, a loss of muscle mass—at the rate of one-half pound per year—is the number-one fitness problem of most women.

So you really do want larger, not smaller, muscles. Larger muscles are your ticket to drop pounds, firm flab, and maximize lean muscle lines.

Larger muscles are the key to combating and conquering your number-one fitness problem.

Chapter 2

Cellulite: Getting Dimpled Pudge to Budge

Cellulite is a popular name for those dimpled, lumpy formations that many women get on their backsides. Usually, it shows up first on the buttocks and then on the upper thighs.

For more than 20 years, fitness-minded women have spent billions of dollars trying to make their cellulite disappear. Few of these women, however, have been satisfied with their results. To better understand why the results have been so dismal, let's examine the phenomenon of cellulite.

Background on Cellulite

The concept of cellulite was introduced in the United States in 1973, the year that Nicole Ronsard wrote her best-selling book entitled *Cellulite: Those Lumps, Bumps and Bulges You Couldn't Lose Before*. Madame Ronsard, as she prefers to be called, notes in the book's introduction that she became fascinated by the word *cellulite* while she was studying in France. French beauty experts supposedly learned of cellulite from Swedish doctors more than 80 years ago. More recently, according to Madame Ronsard, French scientists perfected a way to eliminate it.

The central idea that Madame Ronsard pushes is that cellulite is "a gel-like substance made up of fat, water, and wastes trapped in bumpy, immovable pockets just beneath the skin. The pockets of fat-gone-wrong act like sponges that can absorb large amounts of water, blow up, and bulge out, resulting in ripples and flabbiness you see."

Misinformation Galore

Madame Ronsard believes that cellulite is not normal fat. She therefore claims that typical diet-and-exercise routines have no effect on removing it. What is needed, she says, is a six-part plan involving diet, elimination, breathing, exercise, massage, and relaxation. Since most anticellulite information today involves a variation of Ronsard's plan, a brief overview of each part will be helpful.

1. *Diet*: Avoid foods such as pork, bacon, macaroni, cheese, tuna, and bread, which Ronsard claims leave toxic residues in the body.

2. *Proper elimination*: Ronsard's elimination program consists of drinking six to eight glasses of water a day, consuming a glass of prune juice and a tablespoon of vegetable oil daily, taking a sauna bath twice a week, and having a dry friction rub with a loofah mitten after your daily shower.

3. *Breathing and oxygenation*: Ronsard recommends deep-breathing exercises as a way to oxygenate the body and loosen harmful impurities from the lung tissue.

4. *Exercise*: Ronsard's regimen states that a series of yoga and calisthenic-type exercises must be performed for at least 15 minutes each day, 7 days a week.

5. *Massage*: Ronsard suggests that a woman devote from 20 to 30 minutes a day to kneading, knuckling, and wringing those cellulite-containing areas of the hips and thighs.

6. *Relaxation*: Ronsard emphasizes that when a woman learns to relax her muscles properly her circulation is improved and the release of toxic residues is encouraged.

I've been through Madame Ronsard's book several times. A page-by-page examination reveals that there is little information in the book that is based on scientific fact. Ronsard's six-part plan is not scientifically sound. Nor is it an efficient way for a woman to get rid of her fatty lumps and bulges.

The Facts About Cellulite

Technically, cellulite doesn't exist. You won't find it in any medical dictionary. But the condition to which this word refers does exist.

Most women have thick layers of fat directly under the skin on their upper thighs and buttocks. The dimpled effect is caused by the fibers of connective tissue in the area, which lose their elasticity with age. The overlying skin attached to these fibers gradually contracts. If the size of the encased fat cells does not shrink proportionately, a kind of overall waffling occurs on the surface of the skin. Cellulite is nothing more than thick layers of stored fat that can dimple the overlying skin as the body's connective tissues age.

Proper eating and exercising can definitely have a positive effect on reducing stored fat on the hips and thighs. Such methods as sauna baths, dry friction rubs, massages, deep breathing, yoga postures, pressure wraps, and relaxation techniques, however, do not remove significant amounts of bulging fat. Fat cannot be massaged, perspired, relaxed, soaked, flushed, compressed, or dissolved out of your body. It must be understood and dealt with using scientific facts.

SUCCESS STORY: CARLA BINION, AGE 30, HEIGHT 5'9¾"

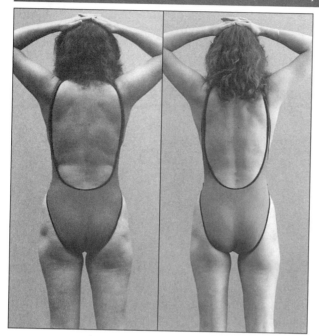

• Lost 18¾ pounds of fat

• Built 3¼ pounds of muscle

• Trimmed 5⅛ inches off her thighs in 12 weeks

"Talk about cellulite! Well, I had it from my lower back down to my midthighs. Now those lumps and bumps have been smoothed away."

Dual Benefit

The next chapter explains why many women tend to store large amounts of fat over their hips and thighs. In the meantime, there is something you can do about dimpled fatty deposits. The solution is twofold:

• You must shrink the size of your fat cells by reducing your dietary calories.

• You must increase the size and strength of the large muscles that compose your hips and thighs.

Body Defining will show you how to achieve both simultaneously.

Chapter 3

Why Women Store Fat the Way They Do

Women and men do *not* live in an equal world when it comes to the amount and concentration of body fat.

Men, with their greater height and larger muscles and bones, are heavier than women. But when it comes to the amount of body weight composed of adipose tissue, women are the fatter sex. The average woman has at least twice as much fat around her hips and thighs as does the average man.

Why do women have more fat than men and, in particular, thicker layers around their hips and thighs? The answer is hormones. Hormones are also the reason that most women have a hard time losing fat.

To understand, combat, and conquer the situation requires a basic knowledge of four related factors: puberty, menstruation, birth control pills, and pregnancy.

Puberty

During childhood there is minimal difference in the body-fat levels between the two sexes. At puberty, however, girls start putting on fat and boys start putting on muscle. A girl must have approximately 15 to 20 percent of her weight as fat before she can start to menstruate.

A low percentage of body fat is the reason some girls who are very athletic—such as gymnasts, ballerinas, and runners—frequently begin menstruating several years later than their more sedentary peers. Often their activity levels must be reduced to allow for normal fat gain, which then kicks into action their hormones and brings about regular menstrual cycles.

Menstruation

Men and women produce hormones that make them characteristically male or female. For women, the two main hormones are estrogen and progesterone. Both can contribute to fatness.

The interacting rise and fall of estrogen and progesterone regulate a woman's menstrual cycle. The entire cycle, from ovulation to menstruation to ovulation, takes from 25 to 32 days.

The same estrogen that is involved in your menstrual cycle also causes you to deposit fat in your breasts, hips, buttocks, and thighs. It does this by chemically stimulating fat cells in those areas to store fat.

Progesterone jumps in by affecting your appetite and mood. It makes you hungrier during the second half of the menstrual cycle and is also responsible for the ravenous appetite that many women have during pregnancy. Progesterone can also make you feel sluggish, sleepy, and less inclined to exercise.

Both estrogen and certain by-products of progesterone cause you to retain fluid. This can make your rings and shoes feel tight during the few days just before your period begins. As you probably know, it's common to gain from 3 to 5 pounds and to feel uncomfortable at this time of the month, a condition often referred to as premenstrual syndrome (PMS). Fortunately, when the estrogen and progesterone levels fall, leading to menstruation, the excess fluid subsides, and the other uncomfortable sensations disappear as well.

Birth Control Pills

Birth control pills are still the most popular form of contraception in the United States. There are different types of pills, but the most popular is a combination of synthetic estrogen and progesterone.

Ten years ago the average woman who took birth control pills gained approximately 3 to 5 pounds of body weight as a side effect. Most of this weight was fat. These pills were fat-producing for the same reasons your body's natural estrogen and progesterone are. Fortunately, most of the pills used today contain much less estrogen and progesterone than the older pills. As a result, the newer birth control pills cause less weight gain.

Pregnancy

Yes, pregnancy is fattening.

Research shows that the average weight gain from the beginning of the first trimester until the end of pregnancy is 27.5 pounds, of which about 20 percent is fat. Your progesterone levels stay high from the beginning of your pregnancy to the end. Instead of making you hungrier for a few days each month, this hormone stimulates your appetite continuously for the entire nine months.

Progesterone is not the real culprit, however, when it comes to weight gain during pregnancy. That distinction belongs to the fat cells, which tend to multiply during periods of rapid growth such as infancy, puberty, and pregnancy. Men and women can also add fat cells any time they gain weight quickly. But with pregnancy, women have a high risk for fat-cell increase that men never have to endure.

The number of fat cells you add depends on how much and how fast you gain fat. Further pregnancies can compound the process. Once a fat cell has been formed, it stays with you for the rest of your life, always demanding to be filled. This is the primary reason why most of the fat gained during pregnancy tends to hang on so tenaciously long after the baby has been born.

Wide, fleshy hips and thick buttocks also facilitate pregnancy and the birth process. A proportional amount of fat usually is deposited around the upper thighs. Many women who have natural tendencies toward these characteristics have an easier time giving birth than do women with thin hips, flat buttocks, and lean thighs.

SUCCESS STORY: CLAUDE HOWELL, AGE 53, HEIGHT 5'5½"

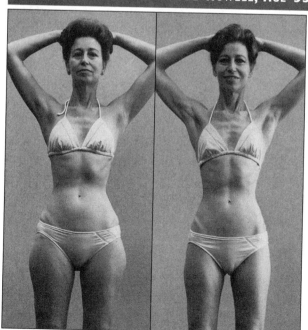

- Lost 21¼ pounds of fat

- Built 8 pounds of muscle

- Trimmed 6⅛ inches off her thighs in 12 weeks

"My goal was to look like I looked 30 years ago. After 3 months, I'm almost there. With all my rebuilt muscle, I certainly feel young again."

Fated to Be Fat?

As I've explained, storing extra fat around the hips and thighs is intimately associated with menstruation, pregnancy, and reproduction. Such fat is a fact of biological life and one that was programmed into the species long ago by nature.

Are most women, therefore, fated to be excessively fat around their hips and thighs?

A majority of women do inherit a large number of fat cells around their hips and thighs for the reasons stated earlier. But regardless of the number, fat cells *can* shrink. You *can* lose significant pounds and inches from your lower body.

Depending on your genetics, however, you may have a harder-than-average time getting lean. If that's the case, you'll deal with the fact best by facing it head-on and realizing that this will require extra time and effort.

If you really want to have a lean body with proportionate hips and thighs, and if you're willing to abandon the quick and easy answers and combat a difficult problem realistically, no roadblocks will stop you. You are not fated to be fat.

You can succeed with *Body Defining*.

Chapter 4

Why Muscle
Matters Most

With proper strength training, almost every woman in the United States can add 3.5 pounds of muscle to her body in only six weeks. What effect will 3.5 pounds of muscle have on your body? You'll find out in this chapter.

Muscle Burns Calories

The general calorie-burning effects of building more muscle were discussed in Chapter 1. Specifically, one pound of muscle elevates your resting metabolic rate an average of 37.5 calories per day.

Resting metabolic rate is the number of calories that your body burns daily in a relaxed state. An average woman, for example, might have a resting metabolic rate of 1,200 calories per day. Add a pound of muscle and her rate would be raised to 1,237.5 calories per day.

In my six-week strength-training program, most women will be able to build 3.5 pounds of muscle. That will amount to a daily increase of 131.25 calories, which is a significant elevation of energy.

Muscles have a vast capillary system. That's one reason why muscles use such a high level of nutrients to remain functioning. A pound of fat, by comparison, necessitates only two calories per day to exist. Muscle, therefore, is 18.75 times more active metabolically than the same amount of fat.

The calorie-burning results of added muscle can have a positive permanent effect on losing fat and keeping it off.

Muscle Moves Your Body

Muscles connect to tendons, and tendons cross joints and attach to bones. When muscles contract or shorten, they pull on bones, and the bones move. Movement of bones results in the flexion and extension of joints.

Although it may seem like an overly simple explanation of what happens to produce movement in your body, muscles are the only things that allow you to move. Hundreds of skeletal muscles can be contracted and relaxed to produce thousands and thousands of simple and complex actions.

Life as we know it is composed of movement. Thus, if you want to improve your life, you must strengthen your ability to move. Proper strength training does that. It can make you a better word processor, piano player, walker, runner, swimmer, dancer, or singer. You name the action or activity, and strength training will help.

Muscle Strengthens Your Bones

Osteoporosis is a condition occurring mostly in women, in which bones become less dense, or more porous and brittle. Postmenopausal, small-boned, fair-complexioned, Caucasian women are in the high-risk group for osteoporosis. The thinning of bone happens quietly without pain until one day there is a fracture or curvature of the spine which becomes noticeable. Approximately half of the women who reach age 75 suffer at least one fracture due to osteoporosis.

Prevention and treatment of osteoporosis involves such things as calcium-rich foods, calcium supplements, hormone therapy, and exercise. By far the most productive form of exercise for increasing bone density is strength training. Common sense reveals that what strengthens your muscles will fortify your bones. In fact, researchers at the University of Florida Center for Exercise Science recently verified this connection. They measured the bone-mineral density of 17 healthy volunteers between the ages of 62 and 82. These subjects were then placed on a once-a-week strength-training routine consisting of four exercises. After six months, these trainees showed an average increase in bone-mineral density of 14 percent.

Muscle Protects You from Injury

Male athletes in sports such as football, wrestling, and basketball have known for years that larger, stronger muscles help protect them from injuries. More recently, female athletes have included strength training in their weekly practices for the same reason. Stronger muscles are better able to withstand all the possible internal and external forces of the sporting event.

Imagine that while riding your bicycle, you suddenly hit an unexpected bump, fall, and contact the ground with your extended hand and wrist. Imagine also that your extended hand and wrist have a maximum strength of 49 pounds and therefore a breaking strength of 50 pounds. In other words, if a force of 50 pounds is exerted against your extended hand and wrist in the right way, then something is going to break. Perhaps it will be a bone in your wrist.

Now, however, imagine that with proper training you double the strength of the muscles that extend your hand and wrist. Instead of having a strength level of 49 pounds, it's 98 pounds. Fall off your bicycle now and be subjected to the same 50 pounds of force on your extended hand and wrist—and guess what? You'll be protected. You might get bruised or scratched, but the bones in your wrist will not break. Fifty pounds of force will not significantly damage muscles and bones with a 98-pound strength level.

It's not unusual for a woman to double her strength in most exercises in three or four months. Some women can even accomplish this in six weeks.

Muscle Works Your Heart

There is a prevalent idea that strength training works only your muscles. To adequately exercise your cardiovascular system, according to this concept, you must do what's popularly called aerobics. Aerobics is commonly described as large-muscle, repetitive-type activities—such as jogging, cycling, stair-stepping, and dancing—that increase the involvement of the heart and lungs for a prolonged time.

Jogging, cycling, stair-stepping, and dancing—if they are correctly performed—do work your heart and lungs at a high level. But so does strength training—if it's done properly.

During proper strength training, you do each movement slowly and smoothly for six repetitions, which take approximately 90 seconds. Then you must move quickly, in 15 to 30 seconds, and start the next exercise. If you keep the time between exercises to 30 seconds or less, your heart rate and oxygen consumption will remain in the target range long enough to increase significantly your cardiovascular conditioning.

Training your muscles and your heart at the same time is much more efficient and effective than dividing them into separate endeavors. Furthermore, it's safer.

Muscle Burns Fat

There is another common misconception among fitness-minded women. It is believed that to shed body fat, you must do aerobics. Doing aerobics, it

SUCCESS STORY: RACHELLE RICHARDSON, AGE 24, HEIGHT 5'10"

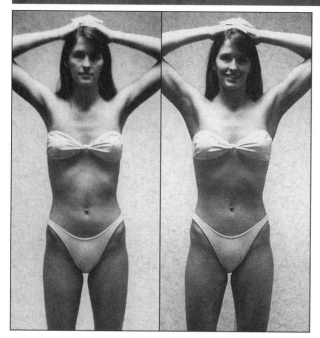

- Built 6¼ pounds of muscle

- Added 1¼ inches on her arms

- Added 2¼ inches on her thighs

- Trimmed 1⅛ inches off her waist in 6 weeks

"I wasn't afraid of getting large muscles, but I was certainly cautious. Once I understood what strength training was doing to my body, I became a believer. Now I want more muscle!"

is thought, burns fat as fuel, while strength training utilizes carbohydrate energy.

What's not commonly recognized is that it really doesn't matter what type of fuel your body is using. The bottom line is that it requires calories. More than any single factor in fat loss, calories count: dietary calories, exercise calories, and metabolic-rate calories.

That's why during strength-training exercise, even though the body relies largely on carbohydrates for energy production, you still lose fat. Those carbohydrates expended during exercise are replaced by foods eaten, and fat stores are mobilized to supply energy needs created by the deficit from your exercise performance, dietary restrictions, and elevated metabolism.

You will make much better use of your time by focusing on your muscles because your muscles will burn extra calories while at rest the next day. That is the awesome body-leaning advantage of strength training.

Edward Jackowski, author of *Hold It! You're Exercising Wrong*, interviewed one thousand women who were enthusiastically involved with aerobics. During the interview, he asked each one, "How many women, including yourself, do you know who have ever vastly improved their body by taking aerobics classes?"

All of them had the same response: "Zero." Not one woman had ever lost a significant amount of fat nor built much muscle from aerobics. Yet, most of these women kept returning day after day and week after week in the hope that something would happen. They twisted, they turned, they stepped, they swayed, and they sweated—but nothing happened.

Why? The aerobics women received poor results because the exercise movements were lacking in intensity. They were not hard enough or progressive enough to produce growth stimulation. Brief, high-intensity exercise is necessary for muscular improvements.

"Do not take any aerobics class," Jackowski concludes, "with the expectation that you're actually going to change your body—because you won't. Take them because you enjoy exercising with others. Take them for fun."

I agree with Jackowski's findings. Even under the best conditions, an aerobics class is not an efficient way to lose fat or build muscle. Anything less than the best conditions produces zero results.

Why not go for the best?

The *Body Defining* plan makes you leaner, firmer, and stronger. You'll see and feel the results after your very first workout. After only 18 workouts, or six weeks' worth of the program, you'll have an extra 3.5 pounds of solid muscle on your body.

Soon you'll know why *muscle matters most.*

Chapter 5

Hard-Hitting Solutions

Avoid secret formulas. Disregard magic pills. Shun wonder diets. Veto comfortable exercises. Forget all the easy claims. They don't produce results.

The valid solutions to your fitness problems are hard-hitting. Accept scientific reality for what it is.

Building Muscle Size

The loss of muscle mass, as detailed in Chapter 1, is the average woman's number-one fitness problem. The solution to this problem is proper strength training.

Chapter 14 will illustrate proper strength training with a tried-and-proved six-week program. This *Body Defining* course can be followed with dumbbells or machines. The course shows you precisely how to perform each exercise for the best results. In a few weeks, you'll see and feel your muscles growing larger and stronger.

Reducing Your Body Fat

Another problem that most women have is excess body fat. While the recommended strength-training program will do a lot to solve this problem, the most effective way combines a reduced-calorie eating plan with strength training. Doing both will guarantee maximum fat loss.

Fatty hips and thighs and cellulite are related to female hormones and the ability to conceive and bear children. The solution to dimpled hips and thighs is to shrink the size of the fat cells in the lower body, which eases the stress on the connective tissue. At the same time, you must increase the size and strength of the large muscle groups that compose the hips and thighs. Thicker muscle, unlike fat, is rigid—and rigidity smoothes the overlying fat, connective tissue, and skin.

SUCCESS STORY: TANYA PELTO, AGE 50, HEIGHT 5'2"

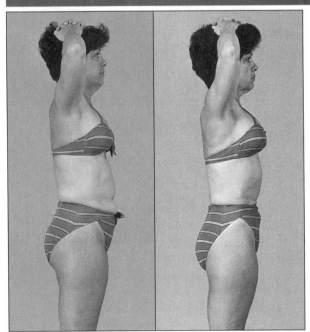

- Lost 18 pounds of fat

- Built 4¼ pounds of muscle

- Trimmed 3⅞ inches off her waist in 6 weeks

"This course taught me how to be in control of my eating, exercising, and total lifestyle."

Counterbalancing Your Hips and Thighs

Body symmetry means having a pleasing balance between your upper body and lower body. Most women tend to be lower-body dominant. Lower-body-dominant women certainly must work the muscles of their hips and thighs to keep them strong and shapely. But, just as important, they must not ignore their upper bodies. In fact, I've designed a special routine in Chapter 16 that shows how to focus on the muscles of your shoulders and arms.

Broad shoulders not only are attractive but also can help a woman become more symmetrical by counterbalancing disproportionately wide hips and thighs.

Remember the fashion trends of the 1980s that emphasized broad shoulders by placing padding in your dresses, jackets, and even T-shirts? This was carried to an extreme by the fashion designers of the popular television show *Dynasty*. They purposely created a powerful, intimidating look by the way they dressed the character played by Joan Collins.

Building the muscles of your shoulders and arms will help to counterbalance your hips and thighs. Soon, you won't need to resort to shoulder pads. You'll have your own in the form of muscle.

Shaping Your Calves

Shapely calves also have a counterbalancing effect on your hips and thighs. When your lower legs are visible, muscular calves naturally draw attention away from your hips and thighs. You can use this to your advantage. Chapter 16 includes an illustrated calf routine that will keep you on your toes.

The Best Solution

To determine the best solution to a problem requires the use of science. Science entails systematized knowledge derived from study and experimentation. For more than 30 years, I've studied and experimented with various eating and exercise plans to help people lose fat and build muscle.

While there are many different programs that claim to provide solutions to women's fitness problems, I believe the ones that I am sharing with you in this book are the most effective and efficient. The proof of the program is in the results, and I challenge any other program to come forth with its data and before-and-after pictures.

I first presented this challenge to a national convention in 1985, after I showed a dozen or more slides of people who had been through a ten-week diet and exercise plan. I've repeated the same challenge many times each year since then. A few people have been upset and have argued aggressively with me concerning their methods and practices, but no one has ever produced data and before-and-after photographs that were more impressive than mine.

Body Defining is the best solution for your fitness problems.

LANGE SKINFOLD CALIPER

Manufactured by

CAMBRIDGE SCIENTIFIC INDUSTRIES, INC.

CAMBRIDGE MARYLAND

Proper use of a skinfold caliper will help you calculate your fat loss and muscle gain from the Body Defining program.

Part II

Strength, Nutrition, and Fat Loss

Using a stopwatch initially will reinforce slow movements during your strength training.

Chapter 6

The Best Style of Strength Training

OK, so you're convinced that muscle really is important for your fitness and health, and that strength training is the best way to build more and better quality muscle on your body.

You must now realize that strength training is much more than simply picking up a pair of dumbbells and moving them up and down and all around. Just as smearing half a dozen colors of paint on a canvas doesn't make you a skilled artist, neither does lifting weights haphazardly get you the body you're after.

The desired outcomes emerge from *how* you put the paint on the canvas and *how* you lift the weight. There are many little things that, when understood and applied, can make the difference between getting great results and not getting any results at all.

The Birth of Super Slow

Ken Hutchins, editor of *The Exercise Standard*, has studied strength training and organized it into a scientific system. His interest in teaching people how to get the absolute best results from each repetition has been an inspiration to me.

Ken and I are longtime friends. We grew up in Conroe, Texas, which is 40 miles north of Houston. We worked together for more than 10 years at Nautilus Sports/Medical Industries. We've planned and conducted—along with Ken's wife, Brenda—many successful diet and exercise programs.

From 1982 to 1986, Ken and Brenda were involved in a large-scale Nautilus osteoporosis research project in Gainesville, Florida. Ken realized early on that when using the Nautilus machines in the standard way—2 seconds on the positive lifting stroke and 4 seconds on the negative lowering stroke—the women subjects had poor control over their repetitions. Two seconds up and 4 seconds down per repetition was simply too fast for their neuromuscular systems to perform safely.

So he slowed the movement, especially the positive lifting phase, where most of the jerking, twisting, and dangerous actions occurred. And he slowed it some more. Eventually, he settled on a protocol of 10 seconds positive and 5 seconds negative. In other words, each repetition required 15 seconds to perform.

Ken appropriately named this new training style Super Slow.® Super Slow subsequently solved the control and safety problems the women involved in the osteoporosis project were having. Furthermore, it allowed Ken to better load the involved muscles, which meant better strength-training results.

After hearing about Ken's progress with super-slow repetitions, I put several male bodybuilders and football players through the 10:5 protocol for six weeks. It's difficult to get experienced trainees to reduce their exercise resistance, which they must do initially to move slowly. Once they all made the transition, however, their results were even better than I had anticipated.

In my most recent book for men, *Living Longer Stronger*, I suggest that men apply a strength-training protocol of 4 seconds up and 4 seconds down. Such a style is much easier to teach men than super slow. But super slow is more productive. It just takes men, as compared with women, a lot longer to get the hang of lifting slowly.

With women, however, super slow is clearly the best choice. Most women haven't fallen into the "how-much-can-you-lift" mentality that consumes many men. Women learn the techniques faster. Thus, I recommend super slow for use in the *Body Defining* course.

In the last several years, Ken Hutchins has organized a Super Slow® Exercise Guild that provides books, articles, and a certification program. You can contact Ken Hutchins by calling (407) 260-6204, or by writing the Super Slow Exercise Guild, P.O. Box 180154, Casselberry, FL 32718-0154.

The Effectiveness of Super Slow

Super-slow training is effective because it eliminates excessive momentum that occurs when you perform fast, jerky repetitions.

If you start with a sudden jerk, then the moving weight can actually pull your body along for the ride, until you have to catch the weight, which is now in the top position. Such fast, jerky lifting contributes to disproportionate, unbalanced strength development. It neglects many muscle fibers and overstresses others. It is dangerous and can cause injuries.

Slow, smooth, deliberate repetitions, on the other hand, involve a maximum number of muscle fibers, which is a key to effectiveness. And once again, super-slow repetitions are much safer than other styles of training.

Doing a Super-Slow Repetition

During a super-slow repetition, you lift the resistance in 10 seconds, then lower it to the beginning position in 5 seconds. The leg extension exercise provides a good example of super-slow mechanics.

Place a light amount of weight on a standard leg extension machine. Sit in the machine with your ankles behind the movement arm pads. Your knees are bent at the start. Instead of lifting the weight suddenly by straightening your legs, do the following:

- Try to move the resistance by only a barely perceptible ⅛ inch.

- Proceed slowly and smoothly once you start moving.

- Continue to straighten your legs and arrive at the fully extended position at about the 10-second mark. Initially, someone with a stopwatch should help you with the counting.

- Pause in the extended top position.

- Ease out of the top position gradually, and return smoothly to the starting position in 5 seconds.

- Feel the weight stack touch, but do not rest or let the slack out of the system. You want to touch, then barely move again in the up-ward direction.

- Focus on keeping the movement arm traveling at a near-constant speed. Do not alternately try to stop and heave into the resis-tance.

- Keep the lifting slow but steady—and the lowering smooth.

- Stop after you've performed 4 repetitions.

Even with a light resistance you should feel a burning sensation in your frontal thighs. Don't be alarmed. The burning is perfectly natural and an indication that the involved muscles are being thoroughly worked.

Practice performing other exercises in a similar manner. Always ini-tiate each repetition ever so slowly. Keep the movement steady.

Super-Slow Guidelines

Super slow can be used with almost any type of strength-training equip-ment: machines, barbells, dumbbells, or even your own body weight. Carefully study and apply the following basic guidelines:

1. Perform three to five exercises for your lower body and five to seven exercises for your upper body, and no more than ten exercises in any workout.

2. Train no more than three nonconsecutive days per week. High-intensity exercise necessitates a recovery period of at least 48 hours. Your body gets stronger during rest, not during exercise.

3. Select a resistance for each exercise that allows the performance of between four and eight slow repetitions.

   • Begin with a weight at which you can comfortably do four repetitions.

   • Stay with that weight until 8 or more strict repetitions are performed. In the following workout, increase the resistance by 5 percent.

   • Attempt to increase the number of repetitions, the amount of weight, or both. But do not sacrifice form in an attempt to produce repetition and resistance improvements.

4. Concentrate on each repetition by lifting the weight slowly in 10 seconds, lowering it smoothly in 5 seconds.

5. Move more slowly, never faster, if in doubt about the speed of movement.

6. Relax body parts that are not involved in each exercise. Pay special attention to relaxing your face, neck, and hand muscles.

7. Breathe normally. Try not to hold your breath during any repetition.

8. Keep accurate records—date, resistance, repetitions, and overall training time—of each workout.

If you use super slow in your exercise performance, your results are sure to be fast.

Chapter 7

Nutrition Basics

Several times a day, you make food choices that influence your body's health. Each day's choices may help or harm your nutritional status only a little. But if these selections are repeated consistently over years, the consequences—good or bad—will become major. Wise food selections now can bring health benefits in the future. Careless nutrition practices can be a contributor to many of the degenerative ailments of later life, including heart disease and cancer.

Of course, a few people will die young no matter what choices they make, and others will live long lives in spite of making poor food selections. For the large majority, however, the food choices they make daily will benefit or impair their health directly. All the energy you require and all the parts of your body are made from the nutrients that you consume in the form of food.

For example, the muscles that made up your arms and legs a year ago have all been replaced by new cells. The fat around your hips last year is not the same fat that is there today. Your oldest red blood cell has been in existence 120 days. The entire lining of your digestive tract is renewed every three days.

To maintain your body, you must continually replenish the energy and the nutrients you utilize. To improve—meaning to reduce, restore, and build—you have to go beyond the maintenance level. To do so, you must understand and apply certain nutrition basics.

Energy and Food

Movement of your body requires energy. This energy comes indirectly from the sun by way of plants. Plants store the sun's energy in their tissues.

When you eat foods such as vegetables, fruits, or cereals, you obtain and use solar energy that these plant-derived foods have stored. Animals get their energy in the same way.

Thus when you consume animal tissues you are eating substances containing energy originally from the sun. Solar energy is initially captured in plants and then consumed by animals and stored in their tissues.

What Is a Calorie?

Scientists measure energy in kilocalories. One kilocalorie is the amount of heat energy necessary to raise the temperature of a kilogram of water 1 degree Celsius. Throughout this book, the common practice of dropping *kilo* from *kilocalories* will be used.

A calorie, therefore, is a unit of measure used to express the energy value of foods or the energy required by the body to perform a given task.

Nutrients

Besides calories of energy, these plant and animal foods also supply nutrients. Nutrients are components of food that are classified into six groups: carbohydrates, proteins, fats, vitamins, minerals, and water.

Foremost among the six groups of nutrients is water, which is constantly lost from your body and must continually be replaced. The energy-yielding nutrients are carbohydrates, proteins, and fats. Proteins, in fact, assume a double duty in that they can yield energy and also provide elements that form working parts of your body tissues.

Vitamins and minerals supply no energy. Some minerals, such as calcium and phosphorus, are major components of bone and other body structures, but all minerals and vitamins act as regulators. They assist in all body processes, such as contracting muscles, digesting food, eliminating wastes, obtaining energy from foods, healing wounds, and growing new tissues.

Some of the nutrients are also labeled *essential*, meaning that if you do not get them from your diet, you will develop deficiencies. Essential nutrients exist in all six groups.

In total, there are more than 40 essential nutrients. Some, such as water and carbohydrates, are required in large amounts. Others—such as vitamin D, vitamin E, zinc, and selenium—are needed in microscopically small amounts.

Whether large or small, the essential nutrients cannot be synthesized by your body from simpler materials. They must be supplied periodically by your food.

Throughout the twentieth century, scientists have made great strides in figuring the measurements of the energy and nutrients that various types of people need. Today they can state with accuracy what your body requires for optimum health and growth.

Nutrient Standards

The Recommended Dietary Allowances (RDA) are applied in the United States as a standard for healthy people's energy and nutrient intakes. These standards, which are revised every five years, cover several pages in the appendix section of most nutrition textbooks.

RDA are set for calories, proteins, eleven vitamins, and seven minerals. There are also estimated safe and adequate intakes for seven additional vitamins and minerals. Estimates can be given for these additional vitamins and minerals, but the data are not sufficient to warrant RDA standards.

The following facts will help put the RDA in perspective:

- The RDA are funded by the government, but the committee that determines the standards is made up of scientists representing many specialties.

- The RDA are based on reviews of scientific research and are revised periodically to include new findings.

- The RDA are not minimum requirements. They are intakes that include a generous margin of safety.

- The RDA are suggested average daily intakes. They are high enough to ensure that body nutrient stores are kept full to meet needs during periods of inadequate intake lasting a day or two for some nutrients and up to a month or two for others.

- The RDA are frequently used to estimate the adequacy of a person's dietary intake over a significant time period.

- The RDA are estimates of the requirements for healthy individuals only. Medical problems may alter nutrient needs.

Separate RDA standards are set for men, women, pregnant women, lactating women, infants, and children. Age, weight, and height are also considered. Despite advertising to the contrary, fitness-minded women do not require superinflated nutrient standards for optimum performance. In fact, the RDA work very well for fitness-minded women.

Food Groups

For many years I taught the four basic food groups to all my trainees. It was a good method for stressing balance and variety in eating. It did, however, place too much emphasis on meat and dairy products.

The new food plan, introduced by the U.S. Department of Agriculture in 1991, centers around a Food Guide Pyramid. Instead of four food groups, there are now six. Fruits and vegetables are now separate groups and a new group called fats, oils, and sweets has been added.

You'll notice that the Simplified Food Guide attaches more importance to grains, vegetables, and fruits than to meat and dairy groups.

SIMPLIFIED FOOD GUIDE

Fats, Oils, and Sweets: use sparingly
Milk, Yogurt, and Cheese Group: 2–3 servings
Meat, Poultry, Fish, Dry Beans, Eggs, and Nut Group: 2–3 servings
Fruit Group: 2–4 servings
Vegetable Group: 3–5 servings
Bread, Cereal, Rice, and Pasta Group: 6–11 servings

Serving Sizes:
Breads and Cereals A single serving = 1 slice of bread, 1 ounce of ready-to-eat cereal, 4 to 6 small crackers, or ½ cup cooked cereal, rice, or pasta.
Vegetables A single serving = 1 cup raw leafy vegetables, ½ cup other vegetables (cooked or chopped raw), or ¾ cup vegetable juice.
Fruit A single serving = 1 medium apple, banana, or orange; ½ cup chopped, cooked, or canned fruit; or ¾ cup juice.
Milk, Yogurt, and Cheese A single serving = 1 cup milk or yogurt, 1½ ounces natural cheese, or 2 ounces processed cheese.
Meat, Poultry, Fish, Dry Beans, Eggs, and Nuts A single serving = 2 to 3 ounces cooked lean meat, poultry, or fish. For example, ½ chicken breast, 1 chicken leg plus 1 thigh, 1 pork chop, 1 small meat patty, or any lean meat the size of a deck of cards. A half-cup of cooked dry beans, 1 egg, and 1 tablespoon of peanut butter each counts as 1 ounce lean meat.

The *Body Defining* eating plan is based on this system. You'll be getting most of your calories from carbohydrates, with only moderate to low amounts of proteins and fats.

The next chapter explains more about the eating plan.

Chapter 8

Body Defining Nutrition

Statistics show that the average woman in the United States eats 2.5 meals a day. She consumes a small breakfast, which is not a full meal, followed by a moderate-size lunch and a larger dinner. In between meals she drinks caffeine-ladened coffee and diet sodas.

Analyses of these 2.5 meals reveal that 46 percent of the average woman's calories come from carbohydrates, 37 percent from fats, and 17 percent from proteins.

The 60:20:20 Breakdown

It is a well-established fact that the average woman's diet could be improved. For starters, she should consume more carbohydrate-rich foods and less fat-containing foods.

The *Body Defining* eating plan stresses a 60:20:20 breakdown each day. That's 60 percent of calories from carbohydrates, 20 percent from fats, and 20 percent from proteins. This is a composition that is ideal for fat reduction, and it also works well for overall health and fitness.

Many women believe that meticulously counting their grams of fat and keeping the total at under 10 grams per day is a must for fat-loss success. This is a misconception. Moderate levels of fat per day produce more effective fat loss than very low levels. Too little dietary fat can cause your body to perceive that something is wrong. Your body may actually start preserving the fat stores you're trying to reduce. In the *Body Defining* plan, approximately 25 grams of fat are in each daily meal schedule.

Small Meals More Often

For efficient fat loss, the number of meals per day should be increased, more equally spaced, and no meal should include more than 500 calories. The *Body Defining* pattern is five small meals a day.

By distributing your food intake into five meals throughout the day you will

- prevent mood changes caused by low blood sugar

- temper food cravings caused by low blood sugar

- reduce PMS and menopausal tension

- eliminate the starvation response elicited by skipping meals

- lose fat because you'll never be putting your body in the storage mode

- experience more energy in all that you do—including your strength-training program

A meal does not have to include a serving from each food group. It can be made up of only one or two. It can be all of the food groups in very small amounts. Even a snack can be called a meal.

The goal is not to eat more food more often but rather to spread your calories into five minimeals a day for efficient fat loss.

Give Up Caffeine and Alcohol

Caffeine mobilizes glucose from your muscles and liver stores and increases the glucose supply to your brain. That's why a cup of coffee, strong tea, or a cola drink makes you feel alert. This may sound positive, but within an hour, your blood sugar levels drop and you feel tired and sleepy. To combat this feeling, you usually have more caffeine, right? Or perhaps you have a high-calorie snack?

Alcohol supplies concentrated calories from carbohydrates, and eventually it will raise blood sugar levels. The initial effect, however, is that alcohol creates a slight drop in blood sugar levels. That means that alcohol can stimulate your appetite, which is one reason so many people have a drink before a large meal. They can eat more!

Besides causing you to eat more calories, both caffeine and alcohol act as diuretics. They both flush too much water from your body.

Invariably, the women who lose the most fat on the *Body Defining* program give up caffeine-containing beverages and all alcoholic drinks. I recommend that you do the same.

Cut Back on Salt

Many women consume diets that contain excessive salt. Salt, which is composed of sodium and chloride, supplies important electrolytes to your body. Too much salt, however, causes water retention. Such water retention is usually in the hands, feet, ankles, face, and abdomen. This leads to a temporary weight gain of three to four pounds, which usually occurs during the last several days prior to menstruation.

Besides influencing water retention, salt is found in many high-calorie foods. Once you start eating foods that contain salt, fat, and sugar, it's difficult to stop. Too much salt, therefore, can be a real detriment to a fat-loss plan.

How much salt is too much? The Food and Nutrition Board's National Research Council recommends 1,100 to 3,300 milligrams of sodium per day for adults, which is equivalent to ½ to 1½ teaspoons of table salt. Most women consume much more than this recommendation per day.

On the *Body Defining* eating plan, your meals each day contain less than 2,400 milligrams of sodium, and that is plenty of sodium for even the most active woman. So hide your salt shaker. You won't need it for the duration of this program.

Chapter 9

Superhydration

A key element to fat reduction can be found in something as simple as drinking water from the kitchen faucet.

Water is basic to all of life. But the old rule that you need to consume eight glasses a day is just that—old. Eight is not enough.

Since 1980, I've advocated what I call superhydration—drinking at least a gallon of water a day. This amount doubles the traditional recommendation. After training more than six thousand women in my various fat-loss programs, I have yet to find a single woman who initially was consuming enough water. They were not dying of thirst—only failing to maximize fat loss and optimize well-being.

Maximum fat loss, optimum well-being, and superhydration are closely related. You are about to see why.

Like an Aquarium

Think of the interior of your body as being like an aquarium—water supports every function. Your body, in fact, is composed of 65 percent water. Besides the free fluids inside your body, muscle is 72 percent water, bone 50 percent, and fat 20 percent.

As important as water is to the composition of the body, only 28 percent of the fluid actually comes from drinking water. Coffee and tea, which are mostly water, make up another 24 percent. The remaining 48 percent comes from milk, soft drinks, meat and eggs, fruits and vegetables, and alcoholic drinks.

The water you drink, as well as the water you get from all foods, mingles with minerals to become fluids in which all life processes take place. An example of water usage in a body function can be seen by examining the lungs. Moisture is necessary to enable the lungs to consume oxygen and excrete carbon dioxide from the body.

According to the college textbook *Nutrition Concepts and Controversies:* "You began as a single cell bathed in a nourishing fluid. As you became a beautifully organized, air-breathing body of billions of cells, each of your cells had to remain next to water to remain alive. Water brings to each cell the exact ingredients the cell requires and carries away the end products of its life-sustaining reaction. The water of the body fluids is the transport vehicle for all the nutrients."

The authors, Francis S. Sizer, R.D., and Eleanor N. Whitney, Ph.D., note that water acts as a solvent for minerals, vitamins, amino acids, glucose, and a multitude of other small molecules. Because it is incompressible (its molecules resist being crowded together), water acts as a lubricant and cushion around joints, and a shock absorber inside the eyes and spinal cord.

It is no wonder that water is second only to oxygen as a necessity for human survival. You can live only a few days without water.

Water is constantly seeping from our bodies. The typical adult emits two to three quarts of water a day through urine, stool, perspiration, and breath. In hot weather or during rigorous activity, water emission is even greater.

The Cooling System

Water is the basis of your body's cooling system—and its air-conditioning unit. Water lost through your skin cools you as it hits the air and evaporates. Water, therefore, is a coolant both inside and outside your body.

The Kidney-Liver Connection

Studies verify that greater water intake contributes to less body fat. This is because your kidneys need abundant water to function properly. When your kidneys are unable to work to full capacity, your liver assumes some of their functions. This diverts your liver from its primary duty—to metabolize stored fat into usable energy.

Fat empties into your bloodstream in the form of triglycerides. Your liver breaks down the triglycerides into free fatty acids, which are usable energy. But if your liver is preoccupied with performing the chores of water-depleted kidneys, it is unable to convert triglycerides. Triglycerides that are not converted into free fatty acids are stored in your body as fat.

Superhydration solves the kidney-liver conflict. But that is not all it does.

Appetite Regulation

Superhydration reduces bingeing and overeating. Water keeps your stomach feeling full between meals. Consuming high-fiber foods accompanied by water magnifies satiation because fiber swells as it absorbs water.

Additionally, it seems that water flowing over your tongue keeps your taste buds cleansed of flavors that might otherwise trigger a craving, particularly for sweet or salty foods. This is not a proven fact, but something that seems reasonable.

Exceed 16 Glasses

The standard recommendation specifies a minimum of eight 8-ounce glasses of water per day, a total of 64 ounces. It's further indicated to include one glass just before each meal and one during each meal.

But it's beneficial to drink considerably more water. Typical women in my fat-loss programs start with 16 glasses and then each week add another two glasses per day. By the sixth week, they are drinking 26 glasses of water daily. The specifics of how to do this are detailed in Chapter 12.

It may help to purchase a plastic 32-ounce water bottle with a straw, which is available in supermarkets and convenience stores. With such a bottle, you can carry water with you throughout the day for continuous sipping.

The participants who consistently drink the recommended water tend to lose the most fat. They also show noticeable improvement in complexion—water helps to bolster skin as its fat cushion departs. Specifically, water buoys your shrinking cells, plumping your skin and leaving it clear, healthy, and resilient.

In addition to preventing dehydration, water is essential to a strength-training program because it supplies muscles with enhanced ability to contract.

Don't Wait to Be Thirsty

Responding to thirst will prevent only severe dehydration. It will not prompt you to drink the water needed for peak performance. Inadequate water intake causes your body to perceive a threat to survival, and thus it begins to retain an excess proportion. Water is then stored outside the cells, resulting in swollen feet, legs, or hands—a condition commonly called water retention, or edema.

The best way to avoid water retention is to give your body its needed water. Only then will stored water be released. If even after drinking 16 glasses a day you have a persistent problem, the likely culprit is excess sodium. The more sodium you ingest, the more water your system withholds to dilute it.

One source of sodium is diet soda. Although free from sugar, the sodium in diet drinks may cause water retention.

Constipation Cure

Another desirable side effect of superhydration is defense against constipation, which is often caused by inadequate water intake. When deprived of water, your system pulls cellular water from your lower intestines and bowels, thus creating hard, dry stool.

One of the key roles of water is to flush waste from the body. This is a substantial chore during fat metabolization because waste will otherwise tend to accumulate during the fat-loss process.

Can You Consume Too Much Water?

You'd have to drink a tremendous amount of water to get too much of it, but it can happen. In the medical literature, such a condition is termed hyponatremia.

I've read reports of hyponatremia occurring in a few athletes involved in triathlons and ultramarathons. Evidently, the athletes consume many gallons of plain water during the course of these unusually long competitions and, because of the continuous activity, they don't or can't stop to urinate. In other words, they impede their normal fluid-and-sodium balance and actually become intoxicated with too much water. Such a condition, however, is very rare.

I've never observed anything close to intoxication happening with any of my participants, and many of them consume two gallons of water daily. Of course, they also have no trouble urinating frequently.

Wash Away Pounds

The benefits of water consumption are vast and indisputable. Don't worry about becoming waterlogged; the more you drink, the more your body will excrete. Soon you'll acquire a natural healthy thirst that helps you maintain your water balance.

Superhydration may be *inconvenient* for a while. But the frequency of your bathroom visits will subside gradually as your system adjusts. During the process, you'll be getting significantly lighter as you wash away pounds.

Note: Anyone with a kidney disorder or anyone who takes diuretics, should consult a physician before making any changes in her water consumption.

Chapter 10

Keeping Your Cool

I f you live in Florida or have ever vacationed there, you've probably gone swimming in one of the many spring-fed state parks. Much of Florida sits atop an aquifer, and millions of gallons of water flow over the surface daily. Almost every Florida state park includes a natural-landscaped pool of flowing water. The water bubbles from the ground at a constant year-round temperature of 72 degrees Fahrenheit.

Seventy-two degrees doesn't sound very cold. But let me tell you, after swimming in the water for as little as 10 minutes—on the warmest summer afternoon—I have remained uncomfortably cool for the next two hours.

Furthermore, by not compensating by consuming high-calorie foods—which would elevate my body temperature—the response to the cold water seemed to draw on my fat stores. As a result, I felt I was getting leaner by the minute.

Research on cold-water immersion shows that my feelings were pretty much on target. In fact, the science of what happens to your body in cold water should influence your attitudes and habits concerning sweating, shivering, exercising, and sleeping.

Cold-Water Immersion

When your body is cold, it undergoes a number of physiological changes to adapt to this stress. The one you are most familiar with is shivering. Shivering occurs when your muscles contract statically to produce heat to warm your body. Ordinary shivering, involving air and not water, can increase metabolism by 20 to 30 percent above normal.

Water, however, has a thermal conductivity 25 times higher than air. Getting into 72-degree water elevates your metabolism much more than does air of the same temperature. Your metabolism will remain significantly elevated as long as shivering continues and for some time thereafter.

Fat provides the majority of energy expended during exposure to cold. And the effect is distributed over the whole body, with absolutely no impact forces.

Exposure to cold also results in increased levels of all the thyroid hormones, and that means that tissue repair, recovery, and growth take place at a more rapid rate.

According to Tom Allen, an assistant track-and-field coach at the University of Florida, many athletes frequent a cold-water (60 degrees Fahrenheit) tank at the university's training complex. "We've found that 15-minute sessions, two or three times per week, speed up healing and recovery," says Tom.

Tom also used the technique to speed his personal fat loss. In one of my six-week programs, he lost 25 pounds of fat and finished ahead of the others in his group, none of whom used cold-water immersion.

Please understand that I am not recommending cold-water immersion as a practical way to lose fat. Shivering can be downright uncomfortable and terribly annoying. Carried to extremes, a person runs the risk of hypothermia—which can cause death.

What I do recommend is understanding the science of how your body responds to cold and using it to your advantage. I want you to apply an almost-shivering condition to your daily lifestyle. I want you to practice being cool.

Drink Cold Water

The first thing you can do to be cool is to make sure that all the water you drink is ice cold. Superhydration results in even more fat loss if the water is approximately 40 degrees Fahrenheit when it is consumed.

Inside your belly, your body has to warm the ice-cold water to core temperature, which is 98 degrees Fahrenheit. Warming one gallon of cold water, which is sipped throughout the day, requires 123 calories of heat energy. Those 123 calories daily can equal a pound of fat loss in less than a month.

It's well worth it to have an insulated water bottle, or an insulated bag to place around your container; your drinking water remains chilled for maximum effect.

Dress Cooler at Work

Many women dress too warmly for their daily jobs. Much of this over-dressing probably goes back to their childhoods, when mothers believed that you should bundle children—especially little girls—to ward off colds. Even today, the average child in nursery school is overdressed in her coat, hat, sweater, mittens, and, beginning in November, boots and snow pants. The overbundled body doesn't learn to use its ability to adapt to temperature changes.

That body of yours, however, is amazingly adaptive if it's gradually pushed in a different direction. Dress lighter. Take off your coat sooner and keep it off longer. Wear short sleeves more often. Don't wear a hat. Open the window wider. Keep a fan on. Turn down the thermostat.

Soon you'll find that what used to be an uncomfortably cool body temperature for you is now quite pleasant. Don't be surprised if you're also leaner.

Exercise in a Cooler Environment

There is little benefit to exercising in a hot, humid environment. Exercise itself causes a rise in your body temperature. To compensate, your body starts sweating. A hot, humid environment makes exercising, sweating, and the cooling process much less effective. Excessive sweating can cause loss of water and electrolytes, and dehydration can result. Remember, one of your goals is superhydration, not dehydration.

In a cool environment, 60 to 70 degrees Fahrenheit, your exercising body dissipates heat easily. That's why it's to your advantage to train in an air-conditioned area that is well ventilated. Some fitness centers that are air-conditioned also use fans as well as dehumidifiers in their heavy exercise rooms. This is ideal.

Be sure to wear brief, cool, well-ventilated clothing regardless of the outside temperature and regardless of how cool you feel during the first exercise. Realize that the longer you can delay the buildup of body heat within your routine the better your workout will be. Don't begin your workout with the notion of shedding layers of clothes as you build up heat. Try not to build up any heat at all.

Avoid Sauna, Steam, and Whirlpool Baths

Sauna, steam, and hot whirlpool baths cause heat buildup and sweating. Sweating does not promote strength building. Strength is developed by exercising your muscles—not your sweat glands.

Your body may weigh less after a sauna or steam bath, but this is due to loss of water. As soon as your thirst is satisfied, your lost weight will return. Sweating does not reduce body fat.

Furthermore, there is no scientific evidence that sweating eliminates poisons from your body. Nor is your body detoxified or cleansed by increased perspiration. Once again, excessive sweating can cause loss of valuable fluids and minerals needed by your system. Minimize sweating.

Sleep Cooler

"Burn fat as you sleep!" That was the headline from a recent advertisement promoting a "miracle pill," which allows you to lose an "incredible amount of fat as you sleep." Of course, the pills and advertisements were taken off the market by governmental agencies because the people behind them had no scientific data to support their claims.

Actually, you do burn fat during sleep. The average woman requires approximately 50 calories per hour while sleeping to keep her body functioning. A typical eight hours of sleep burns 400 calories. And probably half of these 400 calories go to keeping her body warm.

Are you starting to catch my drift? By sleeping a little cooler each night, you can force your body to fire up its thermostat and burn more fat to keep you warm.

If you tend to sleep under thick covers, try to eliminate one or two layers. Wean yourself from using an electric blanket and flannel sheets during the winter months. In summer, pull only a single sheet over you. Then experiment with one leg on top of the sheet. You'll be surprised at how easily your body adapts.

It won't be long till you'll be burning perhaps an extra 10 calories per hour while you sleep. That's 480 calories per night instead of your usual 400 calories.

Don't laugh; every little bit helps. So be cool!

...nn Hocevar   Age: 35

...154   Muscle gained 1½

Total fat lost: **30½**

• Lost 7 inches off th...

Get motivated. Transform your body in just six short weeks!

Part III

Guidelines, Actions, and Plans

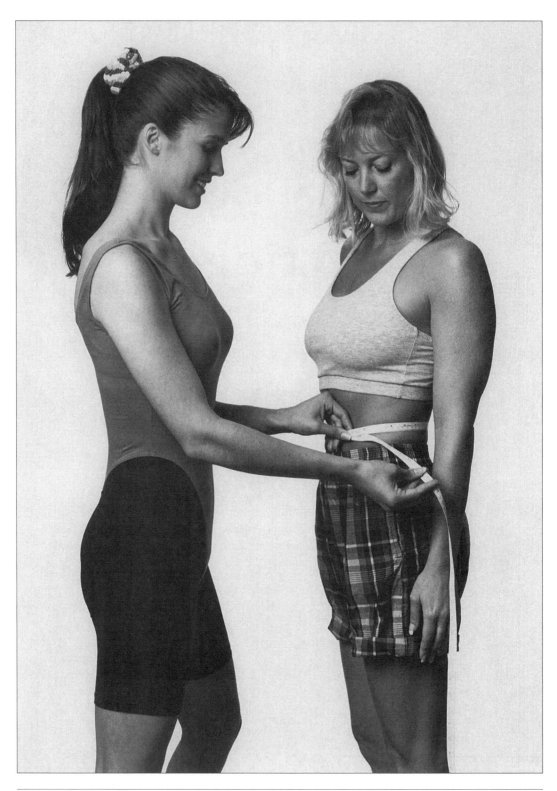

Be sure to measure your waist at three levels: 2 inches above the navel, at the navel, and 2 inches below the navel.

Chapter 11

First Things First

R educed-calorie eating, strength training, superhydrating, and keeping
your cool are salient ingredients in your *Body Defining* program. Before
getting into your day-to-day specifics, there are a few preliminary steps to
take that will make it easier for you to accomplish your goals.

Check with Your Physician

Your doctor should be aware that you are about to modify your eating and
exercise habits. Take this book with you for easy referral. Your physician
will more than likely recommend a thorough physical examination if you
haven't had one in the last year.

There are a few people who should not try the program: children
and teenagers; pregnant women; women who are breast-feeding; women
with certain types of heart, liver, or kidney disease; diabetics; and those
suffering from some types of arthritis. This should not be taken as an all-
inclusive list. Some women should follow the course only with their physician's specific guidance. Consult your doctor beforehand to play it safe.

Do the Pinch Test to Estimate Your Body-Fat Percentage

Since most of your fat is stored directly under and attached to your skin, all over your body, measuring the skin thickness is a way to estimate fatness. Here's how to do a simple pinch test on your thigh:

1. Stand with your weight mostly on your left leg. Locate the pinch site midway between your knee and hip joints on the front side of your right thigh.

2. Grasp a vertical fold of skin between your thumb and first finger. The fold should not include any muscle, just skin and fat. Practice pulling the skin and fat away from the muscle.

3. Pick up a flat ruler in your other hand. Measure the thickness of the skinfold to the nearest ⅛ inch by measuring the distance between your thumb and finger.

4. Take two separate measures of skinfold thickness on your right thigh, being sure to release the skin between each measure. Add them together and divide by two to determine the average thickness. Write this figure on the *Body Defining* Measurements chart on page 66.

5. Estimate your body-fat percentage from the following listing:

Inches	Percent
½	8–13
⅞	13–18
1¼	18–23
1⅝	23–28
2¼	28–33
2¾	33–38
3⅛	38–43

Ideally your skinfold thickness on your thigh should be ⅞ inch or less. This means that your body-fat level is below 18 percent, which is excellent. Within reason, the less fat you have under your skin and around your thighs, the better off you are physically. As your thigh skinfold gets smaller, your arms, waist, hips, thighs, and overall body will automatically develop a tighter, more defined appearance.

Take Body-Part Measurements

It will no doubt be interesting for you to take before-and-after body measurements. Such measurements are best taken before eating breakfast. Remember to enter the numbers on the *Body Defining* Measurements chart on page 66:

1. Measure your height and weight.

2. Take relaxed circumference measurements at eight sites: both upper arms midway between elbow and shoulder; waist at navel, 2 inches above navel, and 2 inches below navel; hips with heels together; both thighs just below buttocks crease. Hold the measuring tape firmly but do not compress the skin. Do not take measurements over clothes and do not exercise before measuring.

3. Determine total fat loss at the end of the program by multiplying percentage of body fat times body weight for the before-and-after tests. For example, it you weighed 140 pounds with 28 percent body fat at the start of the program, that's 39.2 pounds of fat. If you completed the program at 125 pounds and 18 percent body fat, that's 22.5 pounds of fat. The difference between 39.2 and 22.5 is 16.7 pounds of total fat loss.

4. Calculate the amount of muscle gained by subtracting the weight lost from the total fat lost. In the example above, where fat loss equaled 16.7 pounds and weight loss equaled 15 pounds, 1.7 pounds of muscle were gained.

Establish Realistic Goals

Taking your body-fat and body-part measurements will help you determine realistic goals for your *Body Defining* program. The before-and-after photographs throughout this book will also help.

The following averages provide specific pounds and inches lost. They were compiled from the before-and-after measurements of more than two hundred women who have been through six-week courses. Each woman lost an average of:

- 13 pounds of fat

- 2¾ inches off the waist

- 2¼ inches off the hips

- 3½ inches off the thighs

These same women added an average of 3½ pounds of muscle to their figures. These averages provide realistic goals for most women motivated to follow the week-by-week plan. Some women can expect less impressive results and some can achieve greater results—as much as doubling some of the averages.

Use the Tight Pants Test

Another test that I suggest is done with a pair of tight pants. Before you begin this course, squeeze into your tightest pair of pants. You'll probably have to do so by lying on a bed and sucking in your stomach. Stand in front of a full-length mirror and have a good look. Etch in your mind how the pants look and feel.

Take the pants off and set them aside in a safe place. At the end of the program's two-week phases, slip back into the pants for another fitting. If you're following the course strictly, the pants should get looser and looser.

Purchase Measuring Spoons, Cups, and a Small Scale

It's important to use measuring spoons, cups, and a food scale—at least for the first two weeks. It's much too easy to overestimate serving sizes of almost all foods. Read and follow the food preparation directions precisely.

All of the items can be purchased inexpensively at your local department store or supermarket. With food scales, however, you'd be well advised to spend more money to buy a battery-operated, digital scale instead of the less expensive, spring-loaded type.

Swallow a Vitamin-Mineral Tablet Each Day

While on a reduced-calorie eating plan, it's a good idea to take one multiple-vitamin-with-minerals tablet each morning with breakfast. Make sure that no nutrient listed on the label exceeds 100 percent of the RDA. High-potency supplements are not necessary.

BODY DEFINING MEASUREMENTS

Name _____ **Age** _____ **Height** _____

Skinfold

	Before	After	Difference
Right front thigh	_____	_____	_____
Body-fat percent	_____	_____	_____
Fat pounds	_____	_____	_____

Body Weight

Before	After	Difference
_____	_____	_____

Total fat loss		_____
Muscle gained		_____

Circumference

	Before	After	Difference
Right arm	_____	_____	_____
Left arm	_____	_____	_____
2" above navel	_____	_____	_____
Waist at navel	_____	_____	_____
2" below navel	_____	_____	_____
Hips	_____	_____	_____
Right thigh	_____	_____	_____
Left thigh	_____	_____	_____

Chapter 12

The *Body Defining* Program

Afer many years of experimenting with various eating and exercise plans, I've found that most women respond best to six-week programs. Six weeks is not so long that it becomes boring, and it's not so short that she can't see significant changes in her body. Also, I can separate six weeks into three two-week segments—which tends to reinforce subtle, progressive changes.

Almost every day for the next six weeks you'll be using the following guidelines:

Follow a Carbohydrate-Rich Descending-Calorie Eating Plan

Carbohydrates provide your primary supply of energy, as well as a salient source for many vitamins and minerals. On the *Body Defining* plan, approximately 60 percent of your daily calories are from carbohydrate-rich foods. The other 40 percent of your calories are equally divided between proteins and fats. The 60:20:20 ratio of carbohydrates, proteins, and fats is ideal for maximum fat loss.

The eating plan divides into three two-week segments: Weeks 1 and 2 provide 1,200 calories each day; weeks 3 and 4 supply 1,100 calories each day; and weeks 5 and 6 yield 1,000 calories. Notice that the calories get fewer with each two-week period.

This descending-calorie routine ensures against the symptoms that often occur when calorie intake is drastically reduced: an uncontrollable appetite followed by bingeing, a quickly tiring body, and the triggering of the system's survival mechanism that preserves fat instead of burning it.

The *Body Defining* diet offers daily menu selections that are low in saturated fat, cholesterol, and sodium. You'll be surprised by how little preparation is required.

Consume Smaller Meals More Frequently

You'll have five eating episodes each day. You'll have a 300-calorie breakfast, a 300-calorie lunch, and a 300-calorie dinner. With each two-week descent, only your snack calories will change: from 300 to 200 to 100. These calories will be divided into an afternoon and an evening snack.

For each of your five daily meals, you'll have at least three choices. Very little cooking is required. Everything has been simplified for the busy woman.

Keep Menus Simple and Food Substitutions to a Minimum

Research establishes that successful dieters prefer the same foods each day for breakfast and lunch. They like variety, however, for dinner. It may be to your advantage to lock into the same breakfast and lunch foods almost every day.

Furthermore, the women who obtain the best results from the *Body Defining* course almost never vary from the listed foods. I know there are times when some women must make substitutions for certain foods. For example, those of you who are allergic to skim milk may substitute an equal amount of nonfat yogurt. Vegetarians may exchange one egg or a cup of cooked dried beans or peas for one serving of meat.

Drink 1 to 1⅝ Gallons of Ice-Cold Water Each Day

If you're not convinced yet of the importance of water to maximizing your fat loss, go back and reread Chapter 9. Superhydration is a cornerstone of the entire program.

You should begin by drinking 1 gallon, or 128 ounces, a day for the first week. You then add 16 ounces a week until the end of the sixth week. During week 6 you're sipping 1⅝ gallons, or 208 ounces a day. The secret is to spread the water out and drink 75 to 80 percent of it before 5:00 P.M.

Remember, a 32-ounce insulated plastic bottle with a straw for sipping makes the procedure easier to follow. To keep track of your super-hydration, place rubber bands around the middle of the bottle equal to the number of bottles of water you are supposed to drink. Each time you complete 32 ounces, take off a rubber band.

Do Your Super-Slow Strength Training Three Times per Week

You'll be doing three nonconsecutive-day super-slow workouts per week. You'll have a choice of using either machines—such as Nautilus, MedX, and Universal—or dumbbells.

As your dietary calories descend with each two weeks, the number of strength-training exercises gradually ascends. You do six exercises during weeks 1 and 2. You increase to eight exercises for weeks 3 and 4. The final two weeks entail a maximum of 10 exercises.

Practice Keeping Your Cool

It's to your advantage to review often the facts in Chapter 10. Remember, shivering or staying in an almost-shivering state burns several times as many calories as sweating. Besides drinking your ice-cold water daily, practice working, exercising, and sleeping in a cooler environment. Minimize sweating by staying clear of sauna, steam, and whirlpool baths.

Be Excited, Be Patient

Your arsenal is now filled with facts that will help you fight and conquer your fitness problems. You should be ready. You should be excited.

But you also must be patient. Permanent change takes time. The next six weeks will make a difference in your life.

Let's get started.

Chapter 13

Eating Plan: Weeks 1 Through 6

In the past, I've tried all the popular diets, but to no avail," says Nancy Young, age 39, who lost 18 pounds of fat on the *Body Defining* plan. "I always quit because I started thinking about the foods I couldn't have rather than the ones I could eat.

"With *this* plan, however, the foods were tasty and filling—and along with the water drinking—I was always satiated. I had no desire to break the guidelines. Week by week, the inches and pounds just seemed to melt away."

Nancy got such great results because she followed the eating plan and the other recommendations precisely. You should discipline yourself to do the same.

I've tried to keep up to date on the popular brand names and calorie counts, which are listed in the menus. But ingredients are sometimes changed or discontinued. If a listed product is not available in your area, you'll have to substitute a similar product. Become a keen reader of labels. Ask questions about any food or notation you don't understand. Supermarket managers usually are helpful. If they don't have the answers to your questions, they will research them for you.

Begin week 1 on a Monday and continue through Sunday. Week 2 is a repeat of week 1. Calories for each food are noted in parentheses. And don't forget, you'll need an accurate food scale so you can measure ounces or grams. At the end of the chapter is a shopping list for your convenience.

Let's have a look at the menus.

Menus for Weeks 1 Through 6

Breakfast = 300 calories

Choice of bagel, cereal, or shake.

Bagel

1 plain bagel, Lender's Big'nCrusty, frozen (220)

½ ounce light cream cheese (30)

½ cup orange juice (55)

any noncaloric, decaffeinated, no-sodium beverage

Cereal

1.5 ounces (42 grams) is approximately 165 calories.

Choice of one.

Kellogg's Cracklin' Oat Bran

General Mills Clusters

Post Honey Bunches of Oats

General Mills Honey Nut Cheerios

½ cup skim milk (45)

¾ cup orange juice (82)

noncaloric beverage

Shake

Choice of one.

Banana-Orange

1 large banana (100)

½ cup orange juice (55)

½ cup skim milk (45)

2 tablespoons wheat germ (66)

1 teaspoon safflower oil (42)

2 ice cubes (optional)

Place ingredients in blender. Blend until smooth.

Chocolate or Vanilla

1 packet Carnation Instant Breakfast, Ultra Slim-Fast, or other diet shake
  powder that contains the appropriate calories (100)

1 cup skim milk (90)

½ banana (50)

1 teaspoon safflower oil (42)

1 teaspoon Carnation Malted Milk powder (20)

2 ice cubes (optional)

Place ingredients in blender. Blend until smooth.

Lunch = 300 calories

Choice of one of three meals.

Sandwich

2 slices whole-wheat bread (140)

2 teaspoons Promise Ultra Vegetable Oil Spread (24)

2 ounces white meat (about 8 thin slices) chicken or turkey (80)

1 ounce fat-free cheese (1½ slices) (50)

1 teaspoon Dijon mustard (optional) (0)

noncaloric beverage

Soup

Healthy Choice Turkey Vegetable, 15-ounce can (240), or

Campbell's Healthy Request Hearty Chicken Rice, 16-ounce can (240)

1 slice whole-wheat bread (70)

noncaloric beverage

Chef Salad

2 cups lettuce, chopped (20)

2 ounces white meat chicken or turkey (80)

2 ounces fat-free cheese (100)

4 slices tomato, chopped (28)

1 tablespoon fat-free dressing (6)

1 slice whole-wheat bread (70)

noncaloric beverage

Afternoon Snack

150 calories for weeks 1 and 2, 100 calories for weeks 3 and 4, 50 calories for weeks 5 and 6. Combine for appropriate calories.

1 large banana (100)

1 apple (3-inch diameter) (100)

½ cantaloupe (5-inch diameter) (94)

5 dried prunes (100)

1 ounce raisins (82)

1 cup nonfat flavored yogurt (100)

Dinner = 300 calories

Choice of one of three meals.

Tuna Salad Dinner

In a large bowl, mix the following:

1 6-ounce can chunk light tuna in water (180)

1 tablespoon Hellmann's Light, Reduced-Calorie Mayonnaise (50)

2 tablespoons sweet pickle relish (40)

¼ cup whole kernel corn, canned, no salt added (30)

noncaloric beverage

Steak Dinner

3 ounces lean sirloin, broiled (176)

½ cup beets, canned (35)

1 cup skim milk (90)

noncaloric beverage

Frozen Microwave Dinner

Choose one of five recommended meals.

Glazed Chicken Dinner, Lean Cuisine (240)

⅔ cup skim milk (60)

noncaloric beverage

Lasagna with Meat Sauce, Lean Cuisine (260)

½ cup skim milk (45)

noncaloric beverage

Macaroni and Cheese, Weight Watchers (260)

½ cup skim milk (45)

noncaloric beverage

Broccoli & Cheddar Cheese Sauce over Baked Potato, Lean Cuisine Lunch Express (250)

½ cup skim milk (45)

noncaloric beverage

Country Inn Roast Turkey Classic, Healthy Choice (250)

½ cup skim milk (45)

noncaloric beverage

Evening Snack

150 calories for weeks 1 and 2, 100 calories for weeks 3 and 4, and 50 calories for weeks 5 and 6. Combine for appropriate calories. See Afternoon Snacks plus the following:

½ cup lowfat frozen yogurt (100)

2 cups light, microwave popcorn (100)

Shopping List

The quantities you'll need for the listed items will depend on your specific selections. Review your choices and adjust the shopping list accordingly. Remember to check nutrition information on products you buy so that you can carefully follow the menus. It may be helpful for you to photocopy this list each week before doing your shopping.

Staples

orange juice

skim milk

whole-wheat bread

Promise Ultra Vegetable Oil Spread

fat-free salad dressing

Dijon mustard

safflower oil

noncaloric beverages (tea, coffee, diet soft drinks, water)

Grains

bagels, Lender's Big'nCrusty, frozen

cereals

- Kellogg's Cracklin' Oat Bran
- General Mills Clusters
- Post Honey Bunches of Oats
- General Mills Honey Nut Cheerios

wheat germ

malted milk powder

popcorn, microwave light

Fruits

bananas, large (8¾ inches long)

apples (3-inch diameter)

cantaloupes (5-inch diameter)

dried prunes

raisins

Vegetables

lettuce

tomatoes

whole-kernel corn, canned, no salt added

cut beets, canned

Dairy

yogurt, nonfat

cream cheese, light

cheese, fat-free

frozen yogurt, low-fat

Carnation Instant Breakfast packets

Ultra Slim-Fast packets

Meat, Poultry, Fish, and Entrees

chicken, thin sliced

turkey, thin sliced

tuna, canned chunk light in water

sirloin steak, lean

canned soup

- Healthy Choice Turkey Vegetable
- Campbell's Healthy Request Hearty Chicken Rice

frozen microwave dinners or entrees

- Lean Cuisine Glazed Chicken Dinner
- Lean Cuisine Lasagna with Meat Sauce
- Weight Watchers Macaroni and Cheese
- Lean Cuisine Lunch Express Broccoli & Cheddar Cheese over Baked Potato
- Healthy Choice Country Inn Roast Turkey Classic

Chapter 14

Strength-Training Routine: Weeks 1 Through 6

You're going to be really excited once you start building your muscles. I've observed this happen over and over again.

The women in one of my recent groups were given a sixth-week workout with the resistance set back to their original starting levels—and they were astonished at the difference. What had seemed to be a maximum effort six weeks earlier had become ridiculously easy.

Eighteen hard, brief workouts will yield wonders for your muscular strength as well as your appearance.

A 56-year-old woman who recently completed the course marveled that several people around town had mistaken her for her 37-year-old daughter. A few days later the daughter came in to watch her mother train. After mom had progressed through her usual strength-training session, the daughter tried a couple of exercises. To mom's delight, the weights had to be reduced—her daughter couldn't lift as much resistance. "Soon," smiled mom, "with some hard work, you may be even as strong as your dear old mother!" Indeed.

The rest of this chapter reviews important strength-training guidelines and illustrates and describes the recommended machine exercises and dumbbell routines. For better understanding, each exercise illustration highlights the working muscles on one side of the body.

Select the Appropriate Resistance

In super-slow training, you will need less resistance than you would normally use in standard lifting. If you can bench-press 60 pounds for 10 repetitions, decrease the weight by 30 to 40 percent. For example, take off 20 pounds and try 40 pounds instead of 60. This will probably be less resistance than you need, but it allows you to begin with very strict form. The count on each repetition is 10 seconds up and 5 seconds down. This slow style applies to all the standard machine and dumbbell exercises. After several practice sessions, you'll want to increase the resistance on all your exercises so that 6 repetitions of each is a challenging amount.

Work Between 4 and 8 Repetitions

Your guideline number of super-slow repetitions is 4 to 8. If you cannot do at least 4 repetitions, the weight is too heavy. If you can do 8 or more, the weight is too light.

Important: If you can do another repetition, regardless of the number, do not stop. Perform as many repetitions as possible in good form, and then try one more. When upward movement becomes impossible, continue to sustain the contraction for another 5 seconds.

When you can do 8 or more super-slow repetitions on any exercise, increase the resistance by approximately 5 percent at your next workout. This should reduce your repetitions to 4 or 5. Strive to work up to 8 or more repetitions during the next few training sessions. With each workout, you should progress in resistance or repetitions.

Warming Up and Cooling Down

Before strength training, take several minutes to warm up. Do some light calisthenics or ride a stationary bicycle for five minutes. After your workout, cool down by walking around the exercise area, getting a drink of water, and moving your arms in slow circles. Continue these easy movements for three or four minutes until your heart rate slows down.

Machine Routines

For the following routines, you'll need access to a basic set of exercise machines—such as Nautilus, Universal, MedX, Cybex, BodyMasters, or Hammer—which are found in fitness centers throughout the United States. If you do not have access to a listed machine, don't fret. You can easily substitute another machine. Be sure to check with one of the instructors at your fitness center for assistance on how to use any substituted machine.

A Monday-Wednesday-Friday schedule is the choice of most trainees.

BODY DEFINING MACHINE ROUTINES		
Weeks 1 and 2	**Weeks 3 and 4**	**Weeks 5 and 6**
1. Leg curl	1. Leg curl	1. Leg curl
2. Leg extension	2. Leg extension	2. Leg extension
3. Hip adduction	3. Hip adduction	3. Hip adduction
4. Pullover	4. Hip abduction*	4. Hip abduction
5. Bench press	5. Lateral raise*	5. Leg press*
6. Abdominal	6. Pullover	6. Lateral raise
	7. Bench press	7. Pullover
	8. Abdominal	8. Bench press
		9. Behind neck pulldown*
		10. Abdominal

indicates new exercise

Leg curl (for back thighs): Lie facedown on machine. Place the backs of your ankles under the pads, with your knees just over edge of bench. Grasp the handles to keep your body from moving. Curl both legs in 10 seconds and try to touch your heels to your buttocks. Pause. Lower in 5 seconds. Repeat for maximum repetitions.

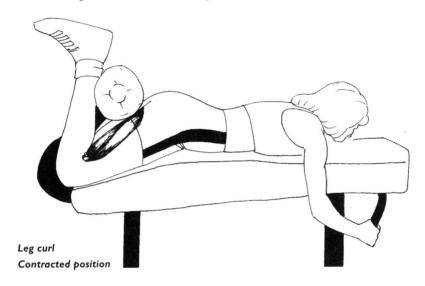

Leg curl
Contracted position

Leg extension (for front thighs): Sit in the machine. Lean forward and place your shins behind the lower pads. Adjust the seat back against your buttocks. Fasten the seat belt across your hips. Keep your head and shoulders against the seat back. Grasp the handles lightly. Straighten both legs slowly in 10 seconds. Pause. Lower the resistance smoothly in 5 seconds. Repeat for maximum repetitions.

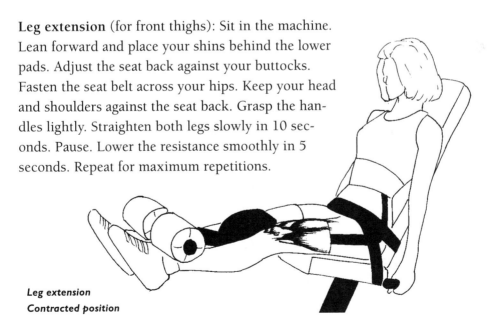

Leg extension
Contracted position

Hip adduction (for inner thighs): Adjust the machine for proper range of movement. Sit in the machine and place your thighs and calves on the movement arms in a spread-legged position. Keep your head and shoulders against the seat back. Pull your knees and thighs together slowly in 10 seconds. Pause. Return to the stretched position in 5 seconds. Repeat for maximum repetitions.

Hip adduction
Stretched position

Hip abduction (for outer hips): Sit in the machine and place your legs on the movement arms. Keep your head and shoulders against the seat back. Push your knees and thighs apart to the widest position in 10 seconds. Pause. Return to the knees-together position in 5 seconds. Repeat for maximum repetitions.

Hip abduction
Starting position

Leg press (for buttocks and thighs): Adjust the seat back and carriage to a comfortable position until your knees—with your feet in the proper position on the movement arm—are near your chest. The closer the seat is to the movement arm, the longer the range of motion and the harder the exercise. Note the seat position and adjust it to the same location each time you do the exercise. Your feet should be evenly spaced apart on the movement arm. Lightly

Leg press
Midrange position

grasp the handles beside your hips. Press with your feet and straighten your hips and knees in 10 seconds. Do not lock your knees. Keep them slightly bent. Lower the weight smoothly in 5 seconds. Repeat for maximum repetitions.

Lateral raise (for shoulders): Sit in the machine facing out. Adjust the seat until your shoulder joints are in line with the axes of rotation of the machine's movement arms. Fasten the seat belt. Pull your knees together and cross your ankles. Grasp the handles and pull back. Raise your elbows to ear level in 10 seconds. Pause briefly in the top position. Lower your elbows and upper arms smoothly to your sides in 5 seconds. Repeat for maximum repetitions.

Lateral raise
Top position

Pullover (for upper back): Adjust the seat so your shoulders are aligned with the axes of rotation of the movement arms. Fasten the seat belt. Press the foot pedal until the elbow pads approach chin level. Place your elbows on the pads and your hands against the bar. Remove your feet from the pedal and rotate your elbows back into a comfortable stretch. This is the starting position. Rotate your elbows forward and down in 10 seconds. Return to the stretched position in 5 seconds. Repeat for maximum repetitions.

Pullover
Stretched position

Bench press (for chest, shoulders, and back upper arms): Lie faceup on the bench, with the handles beside your chest. Grasp the handles lightly. Stabilize your body by placing your feet flat on the floor, or on the step at the end of the bench. Press the handles upward slowly in 10 seconds. Stop short of locking your elbows. Lower the handles in 5 seconds. Repeat for maximum repetitions.

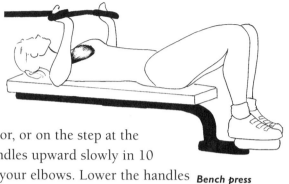

Bench press
Midrange position

Behind neck pulldown (for upper back and front upper arms): There are a number of pulldown machines and bars available. The best choice is one that allows a parallel grip with hands approximately 24 inches apart. If such a bar is not available, use an underhand grip. Stabilize your lower body under the bar. Grasp the overhead bar. Pull the bar slowly behind your neck in 10 seconds. Pause. Return to the stretched position in 5 seconds. Repeat for maximum repetitions.

Behind neck pulldown
Midrange position

Abdominal (for midsection): There are many different kinds of abdominal machines. This description applies to the latest Nautilus version. Adjust the seat so your navel aligns with the red dot on the side of the machine. Fasten the seat belt across your hips. Cross your ankles. Place your elbows on the pads and grasp the handles lightly. Expand your chest, pull gradually with your elbows, and shorten the distance between your rib cage and pelvis in 10 seconds. Pause. Return to starting position in 5 seconds. Repeat for maximum repetitions.

Abdominal
Contracted position

Dumbbell Routines

Even if you don't have access to heavy-duty strength-training machines, you can still build significant muscle with dumbbells and a few calisthenic-type movements using your body weight. The secret is not so much in the equipment but in how you apply what you have available to you.

For the *Body Defining* dumbbell routines, you'll need a pair of adjustable dumbbells and some small weight plates in increments of 1¼, 2½, and 5 pounds. Or you may choose to purchase pairs of solid dumbbells that range from 5 to 20 pounds each.

Use enough resistance on the recommended dumbbell exercises to perform one set of from 4 to 8 super-slow repetitions. When you can do 8 or more repetitions in correct form, increase the combined weight of both dumbbells by approximately 5 percent at your next workout.

BODY DEFINING DUMBBELL ROUTINES

Weeks 1 and 2	Weeks 3 and 4	Weeks 5 and 6
1. Squat with dumbbells	1. Squat with dumbbells	1. Squat with dumbbells
2. Inner-thigh lift	2. Inner-thigh lift	2. Inner-thigh lift
3. Lateral raise with dumbbells	3. Donkey kick*	3. Donkey kick
4. Pullover with dumbbell	4. Lateral raise with dumbbells	4. Wide-stance squat*
5. Bench press with dumbbells	5. Pullover with dumbbell	5. Lateral raise with dumbbells
6. Trunk curl	6. Bench press with dumbbells	6. Pullover with dumbbell
	7. Biceps curl with dumbbells*	7. Bench press with dumbbells
	8. Trunk curl	8. Biceps curl with dumbbells
		9. Triceps extension with dumbbell *
		10. Trunk curl

* indicates new exercise

Squat with dumbbells (for hips and thighs): Place a 2-by-6-inch board on the floor. Make sure the board is long enough to allow you a fairly wide stance. Grasp a dumbbell in each hand, stand erect, and place your heels shoulder-width apart on the board. Lower your body in 5 seconds by bending hips and knees. Do not relax or bounce at the bottom. Return to an almost-erect position in 10 seconds. Do not straighten your knees completely. Repeat for maximum repetitions.

Squat with dumbbells
Bottom position

Inner-thigh lift (for inner thighs): This is a calisthenic exercise that does not use dumbbells. Lie on your side and stabilize your torso. Bend your top knee and put your foot on the floor in front of your other thigh. Grasp your ankle with your top hand. Raise your bottom leg as high as possible in 10 seconds. Pause. Lower your leg to the floor in 5 seconds. Repeat for maximum repetitions. Lie on your other side and repeat for opposite thigh.

Inner-thigh lift
Contracted position

Donkey kick (for buttocks): Here's a calisthenic movement that targets the gluteal muscles. Kneel on your hands and knees. Pull one knee to your chest and slowly extend it high above and beyond your back in 10 seconds. Try to put the bottom of your foot on the ceiling. Lower your knee to your chest in 5 seconds. Repeat for maximum repetitions. Switch knees and repeat for the other leg.

Donkey kick
Contracted position

Wide-stance squat (for thighs): Place a 2-by-6-inch board on the floor. Position your heels approximately 24 to 30 inches apart on the board. Place your hands on your head. Lower your body by bending your hips and knees in 5 seconds. Do not stop or bounce in and out of the bottom position. Return to an almost-erect position in 10 seconds. Immediately, but smoothly, start lowering again. Repeat for maximum repetitions.

Lateral raise with dumbbells (for shoulders): Stand erect, arms at your sides, with a dumbbell in each hand. Keep your elbows locked. Raise the dumbbells to slightly above shoulder height in 10 seconds. Pause. Lower smoothly in 5 seconds. Repeat for maximum repetitions.

Wide-stance squat
Midrange position

Pullover with dumbbell (for upper back): Lie across a bench with your back on the bench and your head and hips off the bench. With both hands, hold one end of a dumbbell over your chest with arms straight. Lower the dumbbell smoothly behind your head toward the floor in 5 seconds. Stretch in the bottom position. Lift the dumbbell slowly back over your chest in 10 seconds. Repeat for maximum repetitions.

Lateral raise with dumbbells
Top position

Pullover with dumbbell
Stretched position

Bench press with dumbbells (for chest, shoulders, and back upper arms): Sit in the middle of a bench. Grasp a dumbbell in each hand. Lie back on the bench and, with elbows bent, position the dumbbells next to your chest. Press the dumbbells slowly above your chest in 10 seconds. Keep your elbows slightly bent at the top position. Lower smoothly, keeping elbows wide, in 5 seconds. Repeat for maximum repetitions.

Bench press with dumbbells
Top position

Biceps curl with dumbbells (for front upper arms): Stand erect with a dumbbell in each hand. Stabilize your elbows by your sides. Curl dumbbells together to shoulder height in 10 seconds. Lower in 5 seconds. Repeat for maximum repetitions.

Biceps curl with dumbbells
Midrange position

Triceps extension with dumbbell (for back upper arms): With both hands, hold one end of a dumbbell and press it overhead. Keep your upper arms near your ears. Lower the dumbbell behind your head in 5 seconds. Do not move your upper arms. Raise the dumbbell to the top position in 10 seconds. Repeat for maximum repetitions.

Triceps extension
with dumbbell
Top position

Trunk curl (for midsection): Lie faceup on the floor with your hands across your waist. Bring your heels close to your buttocks and spread your knees. Curl your shoulders and back off the floor and reach toward your ankles with your hands. Only one-third of a standard sit-up can be performed in this position. Move very slowly in 10 seconds in this short-range motion. Pause in the highest position. Lower smoothly in 5 seconds. Repeat for maximum repetitions.

Trunk curl
Contracted position

Accurate Record Keeping

It is essential for you to keep accurate records of all your super-slow workouts. Make three photocopies of the chart that follows. Each photocopy contains enough space to record your workouts for two weeks. List your exercises for each two-week segment in the left column. Record each workout in the next vertical column, which contains a series of boxes divided by diagonal lines. In the appropriate box, write the resistance above the number of repetitions you complete in good form. Carry your chart with you as you train.

BODY DEFINING STRENGTH-TRAINING ROUTINE

Name   Weeks

Exercise	Date Body Weight					
1.						
2.						
3.						
4.						
5.						
6.						
7.						
8.						
9.						
10.						

Chapter 15

Progress Check

If you've applied the *Body Defining* guidelines over the last six weeks, you should see and feel some major differences in your figure.

Flip back to Chapter 11 and retake your body-fat percentage and circumference measurements. Once you've finished, you'll want to compare your progress with averages I've compiled from more than two hundred women.

Inches and Pounds Lost

If you're typical, your greatest reduction has been in your upper thighs. In my experience, the average woman loses 1¾ inches off each thigh, or 3½ inches combined.

AVERAGE INCHES LOST			
Right upper arm	⅜	Hips	2¼
Left upper arm	⅜	Right thigh	1¾
Waist	2¾	Left thigh	1¾
		Total Inches Lost	9¼

She eliminates another 2¼ inches from her hips and 2¾ inches from her waist.

Waist measurements were taken at three different levels: 2 inches above the navel, at the navel, and 2 inches below the navel. My research shows that some women lose fat from the top down, others from the bottom up, and yet others from the middle out. A three-level comparison helps establish this pattern. For calculation purposes, each woman's largest before-and-after difference from the three levels was used as her waist measurement.

Don't be alarmed if any of your before-and-after differences are less than average. You can measure 20 percent lower and still fall within the normal range. On the other hand, if you have above-average results, you should be elated.

How do these inches translate to pounds of weight and fat?

The average woman who's been through *Body Defining* loses approximately 1.58 pounds of weight and 2.17 pounds of fat each week. Over six weeks, that turns out to be 9.5 pounds of weight and 13 pounds of fat. If you've correctly measured your body weight and body-fat percentage before and after the six-week course, your reductions should be near these numbers.

Muscle Added

In some respects, women have more to gain from proper strength training than men do. Why? Because women have neglected their muscle much more than men. Women are weaker at the beginning stage and they gain strength and muscle at a slightly faster rate.

For example, I've found that the average man builds 3¼ pounds of muscle during his initial six-week program. The average woman builds 3½ pounds. With continued strength training, this same male soon catches and exceeds the female. Hormones are the primary reason.

So you should have built 3½ pounds of muscle as you applied the super-slow protocol to your strength training. And the added muscle is distributed throughout your body: thighs, hips, midsection, back, shoulders, chest, and arms.

Making More Progress

Have you reached most of your goals during the last six weeks? If you are like most women I've worked with, you still want more muscle and a little less fat.

The next section will detail how to continue and improve your results, and how to maintain your new body leanness and increased muscular strength.

As you look back and look forward,
learn from your mistakes and profit
from established facts.

Part IV

Yesterday, Today, and Tomorrow

Be prepared when eating out. Ask for a pitcher of water, decline the menu, and order assertively.

Chapter 16

Continuation

You've made good progress, but you haven't reached your goals. What should you do now?

Answer: Stick with the program. To do so efficiently, you'll need additional guidelines and options.

This chapter opens with some tips on how to make friends, rather than enemies, out of restaurants and holidays. Next you'll learn how to continue with the *Body Defining* eating plan. Then you'll explore two specialized strength-training routines: one for your shoulders and arms, the other for your calves.

Dining Out

The key concept to follow in eating out is to *be assertive*. You must be willing to announce to the managers of your favorite restaurants that you'll carry your business elsewhere unless they provide a greater variety of lower-calorie foods. You must be able to depend on finding diet sodas, sugar and salt substitutes, caffeine-free coffee and tea, whole-grain breads, fresh fruits and vegetables, and nonfat salad dressing in the restaurants you visit. Let the managers know about your intentions.

Here are the best guidelines to use when ordering your meal:

- Request that a large pitcher of ice water be placed on your table. Drink freely before, during, and after the meal.

- Don't open the menu. The menu is supposed to entice you to spend big, and most restaurants know how to sell their rich, expensive specialties.

- Order a simple green salad without such garnishes as croutons and bacon bits. Lemon juice, vinegar, or low-calorie dressing is preferable to any creamy or oily dressings.

- Select two vegetables with nothing added. A plain baked potato is nearly always available. Other good choices are broccoli, cauliflower, and carrots.

- Ask the waiter what kind of fresh fish is available. Though chicken breast is acceptable, you are better off with fish, which is always prepared to order. Because of its lengthier preparation time, chicken is usually prepared earlier in the day with various marinades and sauces.

- Choose a white fish and have it baked, steamed, or broiled, with nothing on it.

- Be very specific with your order. Double-check to make certain that your waiter understands exactly what you want.

- Have decaffeinated coffee or tea for dessert, or at most, some fresh strawberries or raspberries.

Holiday Calories

It doesn't take a math whiz to realize that most people succumb to an avalanche of calories during holidays. Here are a few hints on how to take charge during holiday eating situations:

- Plan ahead, eat ahead. If the festivity includes a meal, find out what is on the menu. If there are not enough good choices, eat at home. Budget 100 to 200 calories for a little grazing.

- Limit alcohol consumption. Alcohol is calorie dense. It also tends to cloud your ability to forgo other high-calorie fare. Never drink alcohol to quench your thirst. Stick to water and ice with a twist of lemon or lime.

- Say no gracefully. You can flatter the hostess by telling her how delicious a particular high-calorie food looks; then ask for the recipe.

- Cut calories when not at holiday parties. During the most tempting occasions, trim a moderate amount from your normal meal schedule. Try to keep all your meals at 500 calories or less.

Commit Again

Let's say that you lost 13 pounds of fat on the program, but you have more fat you want to remove.

Simply repeat the eating plan and practice your strength training for another six weeks. With the same level of compliance, you should be able to get approximately 75 percent of the results. Instead of 13 pounds, you'll lose 9¾ pounds of fat.

Reduce your dietary calories as before: 1,200 for two weeks, then 1,100 for two weeks, and 1,000 for another two weeks. You can continue this down-up-down eating plan for as long as six months.

During weeks 5 and 6 of the initial six-week program, you performed one set of 10 exercises during each of your strength-training sessions. You should adhere to this routine of 10 exercises three times per week until you lose your excess fat.

You may choose to add some variety to your training by trying the specialized shoulder and arm routine, or the specialized calf routine. Both routines are detailed below.

Specialized Shoulder and Arm Routine

In Chapter 5, I mentioned how broader shoulders and more muscular arms can help many women become more symmetrical. Impressive shoulders and arms can draw attention away from the normally dominant hips and thighs.

This routine is best performed in a fitness center where you have available a full line of strength-training machines.

1. Lateral raise, *immediately followed by*

2. Overhead press

3. Biceps curl, *immediately followed by*

4. Negative chin-up

5. Triceps extension, *immediately followed by*

6. Seated dip

7. Leg curl

8. Leg extension

9. Pullover

10. Abdominal

Notice that the first six exercises should be done as three pairs. These paired exercises involve the preexhaustion principle.

The preexhaustion principle requires that two exercises be performed back-to-back with minimal rest between. The first exercise is a single-joint movement that targets a specific muscle. The second exercise involves multiple joints, which bring into action surrounding muscles that force the targeted muscle to a deeper level of fatigue.

Super slow is the suggested style to use in this new routine for the shoulders and arms. Here are guidelines for you to follow.

Lateral raise (for shoulders): Sit in the lateral raise machine and make the necessary adjustments. Do as many super-slow repetitions as you can in proper form. Doing so will isolate your deltoids or shoulder muscles and leave them in a state of preexhaustion. Instead of resting for 15 to 30 seconds as you walk to your next exercise, you must move quickly—in less than 3 seconds—to the overhead press machine. Fortunately, in most fitness centers, the overhead press machine is next to the lateral raise.

Lateral raise
Top position

Overhead press (for shoulders and back upper arms): Sit in the machine with the handles beside your shoulders. Grasp the handles, keep your back straight, and cross your ankles. In 10 seconds, press the handles to the full overhead position. Lower the handles smoothly in 5 seconds. After several repetitions, you'll feel an intense burn throughout your shoulders, but don't stop. Grind out as many as you can. When you can do no more, take a two-minute rest. During that period you'll experience what bodybuilders commonly call a *pump*. A pump is an extraordinary amount of blood that forces into a working muscle

Overhead press
Midrange position

within a short period of time. It gives you a feeling that the targeted muscle is significantly bigger. And it is, but it's only temporary. It will gradually—within several minutes—return to normal. Still, it is a valuable preview of even better results.

Biceps curl (for front upper arms): It's best to have an instructor in your fitness center help you do the biceps curl and negative chin-up. Sit in the biceps curl machine with your elbows in line with the rotation points of the movement arms. Grasp the handles with your palms up. Curl the handles to your shoulders in 10 seconds. Pause. Lower smoothly in 5 seconds. Repeat for 4 to 8 repetitions. After your final repetition, run to a horizontal bar for chin-ups.

Biceps curl
Midrange position

Negative chin-up
Top position

Negative chin-up (for front upper arms and upper back): Negative means you'll be doing only the lowering part of a chin-up. Instead of trying to pull yourself up, which most women have difficulty accomplishing, you'll climb to the top position. This exercise is best executed on the Nautilus multi-exercise machine. Lower the carriage so you can easily get your chin over the crossbar, which should be in the forward placement. Grasp the crossbar with an underhand grip. Climb to the top position until your chin is above the crossbar. Stabilize your elbows near your torso and take your feet off the steps. You should now be holding your body weight with your arms. Once again, it's a good idea to have an instructor handy to assist and talk you through this movement. Your goal is to lower your body slowly in 10 seconds until your elbows are straight. Climb back to the top, reposition your chin over the bar, and repeat. Try to do 4 to 8 slow repetitions. This is a difficult exercise to master. But if you can learn it, it will do wonders for your biceps and torso muscles.

Triceps extension (for back upper arms): I prefer using the Nautilus version of this machine. Sit in the machine with your elbows on the padded bench and your hands in front of the movement arms. Your shoulders should be at the same level as your elbows. Straighten your arms slowly in 10 seconds by pushing on the movement arms. Pause. Return smoothly to the stretched position in 5 seconds. Repeat for maximum repetitions. After your final repetition, exit the machine, and quickly move to the seated dip machine.

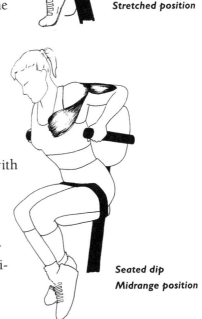

Triceps extension
Stretched position

Seated dip (for back upper arms, shoulders, and chest): The seated dip machine now allows your chest muscles, which are rested, to push your triceps, which are preexhausted, to a deep state of fatigue. Sit in the machine with the handles near your armpits. Place your hands on top of the handles. Press the handles downward slowly in 10 seconds. Allow the handles to rise in 5 seconds for a comfortable stretch. And, as always, do as many repetitions as you possibly can. At the end, your triceps should be well pumped.

Seated dip
Midrange position

Complete the routine by working on the leg curl, leg extension, pullover, and abdominal machines—with a normal amount of rest between them all.

You can repeat the entire routine three times a week for two weeks. Then you'll need to go back to your previous program. Or you can experiment with the specialized calf routine.

Specialized Calf Routine

Your lower leg is composed of twelve muscles. The most important are the gastrocnemius and soleus of your back calf and the tibialis anterior of your front calf. To work these muscles thoroughly, four exercises are required. You do *not* have to rush in a preexhaustion manner between any of them. Here's the way to do each in the super-slow style.

1. Standing calf raise

2. One-legged calf raise

3. Seated calf raise

4. Front-toe raise

5. Hip abduction

6. Leg press

7. Lateral raise

8. Pullover

9. Bench press

10. Behind neck pulldown

Standing calf raise (for back calves): This exercise can be performed on a variety of machines. Stand under the machine, or place the weighted belt around your hips, lift the movement arm with your legs, and position the balls of your feet securely on the bottom block or step. Straighten your knees and keep them locked throughout the movement. Raise your heels slowly in 10 seconds and try to stand on your tiptoes. Pause. Lower your heels smoothly in 5 seconds to a deep stretch. Repeat for maximum repetitions.

Standing calf raise
Contracted position

One-legged calf raise (for back calves): This movement requires no machine, only your body weight. In a standing position, place the ball of your right foot on a block or step. Bend your left knee and lift your left foot from the floor. Use your arms and hands to stabilize your body. While keeping your right knee locked, raise and lower your heel in the super-slow manner. When your right calf fatigues, switch to your left leg and repeat the process with your left calf.

One-legged calf raise
Contracted position

Seated calf raise (for side calves): Sit in the machine with your knees bent. Adjust the padded movement arm so your knees and thighs fit snugly underneath. Only the balls of your feet should be on the lower step. Raise your heels in 10 seconds. Pause. Lower smoothly in 5 seconds. Repeat for as many repetitions as possible.

Seated calf raise
Contracted position

Front-toe raise (for front calves): You'll feel this exercise over your front calves and shins. No machine is necessary. Stand with your back against a smooth wall. Walk your heels out approximately 18 inches from the wall. Lock your knees and keep them locked. Your weight should be distributed on your heels and buttocks as you lean back into the wall. Slowly raise the front of your feet and toes as high above the floor as possible. Lower smoothly. Repeat for maximum repetitions.

Front-toe raise
Contracted position

Finish the rest of your workout by doing six other exercises: hip abduction, leg press, lateral raise, pullover, bench press, and behind neck pulldown. As with the shoulder and arm routine, I'd recommend that you try the calf routine for two weeks. Then go back to your regular routine. You may choose to do a specialization cycle again in three months.

Continue Other Practices

While you're improving your results, your other practices—such as superhydration, avoiding stress, and sleeping cool—should remain the same as during weeks 5 and 6.

Your goals, if they are realistic, are only a few weeks away. Stay on course.

Chapter 17

Maintenance

Most women in my programs reach their initial goals in six to twelve weeks. A few, however, take as long as six months. Once you become satisfied with the condition of your body, your next priority is to understand maintenance. Successful maintenance requires some minor adjustments to the practices that you've been adhering to for the last several months.

Follow a Carbohydrate-Rich Moderate-Calorie Eating Plan

Carbohydrate-rich meals are still what you should be consuming, but your total calories per day can be increased. Instead of taking in from 1,000 to 1,200 calories a day, you should eat from 1,400 to 2,100 calories per day.

You can figure out your maintenance calorie level by gradually adding calories back into your eating plan. For example, you try a certain level—say 1,500 calories a day—for two weeks. Careful weighings reveal that you are still losing a little fat. So you raise your calories to 1,700 calories a day for another two weeks and your body weight remains constant. Now you know that you've reached the upper limit of your maintenance calorie level.

Remember to refer back to Chapter 7 and the Simplified Food Guide for suggestions on the 60:20:20 ratio of carbohydrates, proteins, and fats. Remember, fruits, vegetables, breads, and cereals are your primary sources of carbohydrates.

Eat Smaller Meals More Frequently

You've been limiting your five meals per day to 300 calories or less. To maintain your body weight, set the limit per meal to 400 calories or less most of the time. A 500-calorie meal is even OK once in a while. Anything bigger than 500 calories probably means that your body will be storing the excess in your fat cells.

SUCCESS STORY: SYBIL KING, AGE 27, HEIGHT 5'7"

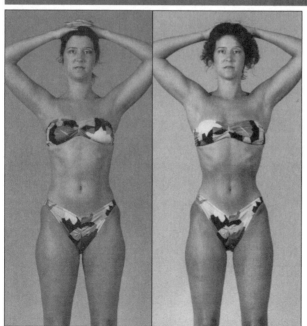

- Lost 14½ pounds of fat

- Built 3½ pounds of muscle

- Trimmed 3 inches off her waist in 6 weeks

"I went through the six-week program in 1988 and it got me into great shape fast. Now, more than seven years later, I'm still practicing the simple guidelines to maintain my muscle-to-fat ratio."

Even if that happens, don't panic. Simply anticipate, plan, and get back on your schedule.

Drink 1 Gallon of Cold Water Each Day

You've experienced the positive effects of sipping plenty of cold water each day. You should now understand the importance of superhydration in fat loss, muscle building, skin health, and internal and external cooling. Water supports your every function.

Make superhydration—the drinking of at least 1 gallon of cold water a day—a permanent part of your new lifestyle.

Strength Train Twice a Week

You must continue to strength train your newly built muscles or they will shrink. Don't allow this wasting away to happen to your lean, defined body. Remember, strong and shapely muscles are one of your best insurance policies against regaining fat.

The primary difference between muscle maintenance and muscle building is that you don't need to train as often. Your frequency of training may be reduced from three to two times per week. Most women on my maintenance programs work out on Mondays and Thursdays.

Keep in mind that *more* exercise is not *better* exercise. Better exercise is *slower* and *harder*. Apply this concept consistently and the leanness and muscular definition of your body may well exceed your goals.

Chapter 18

Lose 7 Pounds in 10 Days

This chapter is for women who occasionally backslide by overeating, neglecting their water drinking, failing to exercise, or any combination of these practices.

For example, between Thanksgiving and New Year's Day, many people go bonkers and gain 7 or more pounds of fat. Excessive fat gain is a key reason why January is traditionally the busiest month for fitness clubs and diet centers.

In addition, some women can get sidetracked by food cravings. One woman, who had been through twelve weeks of the program and had lost 21 pounds of fat, came to see me after having missed almost a month of workouts.

"It was the chocolate," she said. "I hadn't had any in three months. Then one day I park my car on the opposite side of the supermarket where I shop. There's a little candy shop that just opened.

"And you know what? The smell of that warm chocolate just drew me right in. The next thing I know, I'm savoring a sample. I must've eaten almost a box right there.

"I promptly spent my shopping money on chocolate: dark, light, plus the kinds with nuts and cherries. Next week I felt so ashamed that I just stopped working out and started eating more of all the foods I knew I shouldn't be eating."

This chapter is also for women who are too embarrassed by recent weight gain to work out at their local fitness center and would like to make a little progress at home before allowing friends at the fitness center to see them again.

Whether your weakness is Thanksgiving, Christmas, chocolate, or anything else related to eating and exercising, this chapter may provide you with the quick-start program and motivation you need to get you back to your eating plan and back to the gym.

It's called "Lose 7 Pounds in 10 Days," and that's exactly what happened to my initial test group of women who went through this plan at the Gainesville Health & Fitness Center. Each woman lost an average of 7.7 pounds of fat, 2.56 inches off her waist, and 1.75 inches off her thighs. That's quite an accomplishment for only 10 days of discipline.

SUCCESS STORY: ELENA WELSH, AGE 38, HEIGHT 5'10"

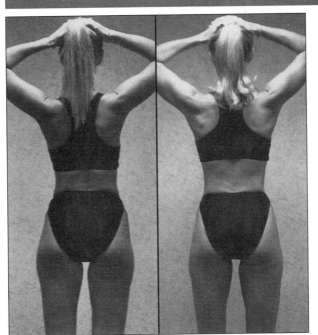

• Lost 8¾ pounds of fat

• Built 1 pound of muscle

• Trimmed 2¼ inches off her thighs in 10 days

"Everything just seemed to click—the simple eating plan, the cold water, and the at-home exercise routine—and my winter pudge disappeared. All my freinds noticed the difference immediately. I've been on a roll ever since."

You'll recognize most of the foods and some of the exercises from the *Body Defining* program. In fact, the major guidelines that you are familiar with have been condensed to the following three steps.

Step 1: Eat 1,100 Calories Each Day

Breakfast = 300 Calories

> 1 plain bagel, Lender's Big'nCrusty, frozen (220)
>
> ½ ounce light cream cheese (30)
>
> ½ cup orange juice (55)
>
> any beverage without calories, caffeine, or sodium, such as decaffeinated coffee or tea.

Lunch = 300 Calories

> Make a sandwich consisting of:
>
> 2 slices whole-wheat bread (140)
>
> 2 teaspoons Promise Ultra Vegetable Oil Spread (24)
>
> 2 ounces white meat (about 8 thin slices), chicken or turkey (80)
>
> 1 ounce fat-free cheese (1½ slices) (50)
>
> 1 teaspoon Dijon mustard (optional) (0)
>
> non-caloric beverage

Afternoon Snack = 100 Calories

> Choice of 1 apple (100) or 1 cup nonfat flavored yogurt (100)

Dinner = 300 Calories

> *Choice of one of three meals:*
>
> ### Glazed Chicken Dinner, Lean Cuisine (240)
>
> ⅔ cup skim milk (60)
>
> noncaloric beverage

Lose 7 Pounds in 10 Days 113

Lasagna with Meat Sauce, Lean Cuisine (260)
½ cup skim milk (45)
noncaloric beverage

Country Inn Roast Turkey Classic, Healthy Choice (250)
½ cup skim milk (45)
noncaloric beverage

Evening Snack = 100 Calories
Choice of 1 apple (100) or 1 cup nonfat flavored yogurt (100)

Step 2: Emphasize Superhydration

If you aren't drinking at least five quarts of ice-cold water each day, do so every day for the next 10 days.

Superhydration speeds fat loss, helps muscle building and recovery, increases circulation, combats constipation, and moisturizes your skin.

Don't leave home without your water bottle.

Step 3: Follow a Brief At-Home Strength-Training Routine

If you haven't been strength training consistently for several weeks or more, your body weight will probably provide sufficient resistance to your muscles for 10 days.

Use only one set of five exercises. Perform them every other day. Begin with 4 repetitions and work up to 8 repetitions or more. Do them all slowly according to the following instructions.

Side bend (for sides of waist): Stand with feet hip-width apart, elbows extended, and hands clasped overhead. Reach toward the ceiling and smoothly bend laterally to the left. Pause briefly in the stretched position

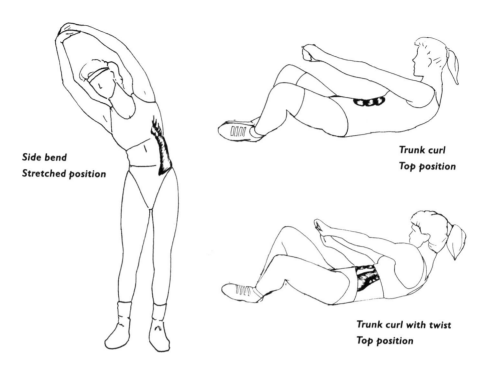

Side bend
Stretched position

Trunk curl
Top position

Trunk curl with twist
Top position

and reach again with your arms. The bending should take 5 seconds. Return slowly to the top center position in 10 seconds. Do not let your hands move forward. Keep them directly over the middle of your head. Reach toward the ceiling with both hands and repeat bending to the left side for the required repetitions. Perform the same number of repetitions on the right side.

Trunk curl (for midsection): Lie faceup on the floor with your hands across your waist. Bring your heels close to your buttocks and spread your knees. Curl your shoulders and back off the floor and reach your hands toward your ankles. Move very slowly in 10 seconds in this short-range motion. Pause in the highest position. Lower under control in 5 seconds. Repeat for the required repetitions.

Trunk curl with twist (for middle and sides of waist): Assume the same position as for the trunk curl. Curl your shoulders gradually off the floor in 10 seconds and reach your hands toward your left knee. In

the top position twist with your torso to
your right knee. Lower your shoulde
onds. Repeat movement, but this
twist to the left, and lower. Al'
twisting for required repetit'

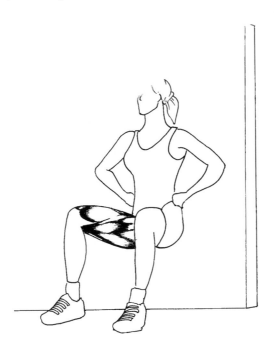

Wall squat
Bottom position

Wall squat (for buttocks and thighs): Stand erect and lean back against a
smooth, sturdy wall. Place your heels 3 inches wider apart than your hips
and approximately 12 inches away from the wall. Place your hands on your
hips and slide your back down the wall until the tops of your thighs are
parallel to the floor. Hold for 10 seconds. Push back to the top position
and immediately lower to the parallel position. Do not lock your knees in
the top position; keep them slightly bent. Repeat for six sustained-contrac-
tion repetitions. Increase the duration of each repetition by 5 seconds each
workout. Your goal is to do six 30-second repetitions.

Negative push-up (for chest, shoulders, and backs of upper arms): In this
exercise you'll do a negative, or lowering-only, movement. Assume a stan-

Negative push-up
Midrange position

dard push-up position—on your toes and hands with body stiff. Your hands should be under your shoulders with elbows locked. Lower your body to the floor by bending your arms slowly in 10 seconds. Do not try to push yourself up to the top position. When you reach the floor, bend your knees, get back on your toes, and stiffen your body once again. Repeat for 4 lowering repetitions. Add 1 repetition per workout.

Chapter 19

Questions, Please

The following questions and answers should help fill in any remaining gaps about the *Body Defining* program. Among the women participating in the plan, these concerns have been common.

How to Breathe

I'm confused about how to breathe during the super-slow strength training.

The proper breathing technique for each super-slow exercise is as follows:

- Breathe normally during the first and second repetitions.

- Remind yourself to take short, shallow breaths when breathing becomes more difficult. This usually occurs during the third and fourth repetitions and persists until the final repetition is completed.

- Do not hold your breath on any repetition. Remain alert and breathe.

- Emphasize exhalation more than inhalation, especially during the last two repetitions.

Muscle Turning to Fat

If I build too much muscle, won't it eventually turn to fat?

There is some confusion here. It's common to refer to an overweight woman as "fat," when in fact she does have other components—such as muscle, bone, and organs—in her body. Likewise, a lean woman is said to be "all muscle," which technically doesn't mean she is devoid of fat. She simply has a low percentage of body fat.

It should be clearly understood that muscle doesn't ever turn to fat. Fat and muscle cells are very different. The chemistry of each won't allow a change of one to the other.

As I pointed out in Part I, both fat cells and muscle cells have the capacity to inflate or deflate. The average woman, once again, has too much fat and too little muscle. The goal of *Body Defining* is to decrease the size of your fat cells and increase the size of your muscle cells.

How Fat Leaves the Body

What happens to the fat I lose? How does it get out of my body and where does it go?

The science behind the fat-loss process is interesting as well as misunderstood. Fat is energy and energy is best expressed in calories, which are units of heat measurement. Remember, one pound of body fat contains 3,500 calories. Your body gets rid of fat or calories in three ways: through your skin, through your lungs, and through elimination of fluids as urine.

Surprisingly, most of the calories are eliminated through your skin. Your skin is your body's largest organ, and as much as 85 percent of your daily energy emerges through it as heat. You lose heat through your skin by radiation, conduction, convection, and evaporation.

Radiation is the most important of these and it's the reason a tall woman has an easier time losing fat than a shorter woman of the same weight. The taller woman generally has more skin than the shorter woman and thus she is able to radiate more heat to the environment.

Conduction is the transfer of calories through direct contact. Conduction is why cold-water immersion (described in Chapter 10) and the concept of remaining cool are valid ways to eliminate calories.

Heat also exits through your lungs and through warm urine. Exercise increases your respiratory rate, and that is helpful. Superhydration directly increases your volume of urine, and that is another significant, mostly ignored, way of generating heat loss.

Years ago Albert Einstein and others proved that you cannot create or destroy energy; you can only transfer it. Thus, fat transfers out of your body where it is put to use by other living organisms and by the environment. With each use, there is a transfer, and the cycle continues endlessly.

SUCCESS STORY: SHANAN STEWART, AGE 23, HEIGHT 5'5½"

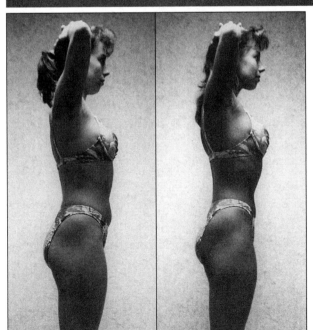

• Lost 10 pounds of fat

• Built 2 pounds of muscle

• Trimmed 4¾ inches off her waist in 6 weeks

"Even though I worked at a fitness center for the last three years, I wasn't consistent with my eating and exercising. Furthermore, they both lacked intensity. The *Body Defining* plan pulled it all together for me."

Why No Aerobics?

Why are there no aerobic exercises included in the Body Defining *plan?*

I touched on this briefly in Chapter 4. To answer this question thoroughly, however, requires an examination of three definitions of the word *aerobic*.

First, *aerobic* generally relates to an activity that involves an increased participation of the heart and lungs over a prolonged period of time. If the heart rate doubles when you run across a busy intersection and then returns to normal after a few seconds or minutes, the activity is anaerobic, or *not* aerobic. If the activity is continued long enough at an adequate pace to sustain an elevated heart rate for many minutes, then it is said to be aerobic.

Second, biochemists classify your energy-producing metabolic pathways as aerobic and anaerobic. Aerobic refers to the presence of oxygen, whereas *anaerobic* means without oxygen.

Third, *aerobics* to many people means whole-body dance movements that are performed in a group setting to popular music. Jacki Sorensen and Jane Fonda popularized this form of dancing in the 1980s. More recently it has been promoted in videos by Kathy Smith, Gin Miller, Candice Copeland, and Kari Anderson.

The *Body Defining* strength-training program can involve your heart, lungs, and metabolic system aerobically—according to the first and second definitions. To do this, however, you must be skilled in the use of the exercise equipment, be strong enough to elevate your heart rate from 70 to 85 percent of your maximum level, and be enduring enough to move quickly from one machine to the next in 15 seconds or less.

During the last two weeks of the program, it is easily possible to keep your heart rate from 70 to 85 percent of your maximum level for 15 to 20 minutes, which satisfies the major requirement for cardiovascular endurance. During the super-slow workout, your leg and arm muscles (depending on the specific exercise) are involved anaerobically. But your core torso muscles—the abdominal and erector spinae, for example—are working aerobically because they are required for stabilization during each exercise.

I do not recommend that you combine strength training with aerobic-dance movements. Aerobic dancing—and other activities such as running, swimming, cycling, and racquetball—do not contribute significantly to the fat-loss process. In fact, when added to the program these activities can actually retard the loss of fat.

Fat loss is retarded in two ways. Too much repetitive activity prevents maximum muscle building by using up your recovery ability. Unimpaired recovery ability is necessary for muscular growth. Too much activity—especially if you're on a reduced-calorie diet—causes you to get the blahs and quickly lose your enthusiasm. If this happens, you're sure to go off your eating plan.

A major purpose of the *Body Defining* program is to help you lose fat in the most effective and most efficient manner possible. Fat loss is prioritized and maximized by building muscle at the same time. The muscle-building process is optimized by unimpaired recovery ability. Unimpaired recovery ability depends on keeping your strenuous and moderately strenuous activities to a bare minimum.

Once you get your body fat to a low level, you can add other activities to your weekly fitness schedule—and I encourage you to do so. If you wish to do both, perform strength training and aerobics on the same day and rest the day after. But for now, you should follow the program exactly as directed.

So you're saying that strength training does involve aerobic conditioning?

Yes, the recommended super-slow exercise certainly has the capacity to provide aerobic conditioning—if you are skilled enough, strong enough, and enduring enough to perform each exercise properly. Doing each exercise slowly and then moving quickly between machines will keep your heart rate elevated to the desired level for 15 to 20 minutes. It will also work your core torso muscles continuously for the duration of the workout. Furthermore, because the exercise is performed slowly and smoothly, it is very safe compared with aerobic dancing and jogging.

Flexibility

I've always liked doing stretching movements to improve my flexibility. Can I supplement the Body Defining *plan with stretching?*

For years stretching movements have been used almost as a cure-all. Women have been told that stretching will improve flexibility, firm and shape the body, reduce fat, and prevent injuries. As a result, women by the thousands stretch their bodies in organized classes at local clubs or in front of television instructors at home, with and without various types of music.

Most women are attracted to stretching movements simply because they are easy, fun, and social, especially since large groups can be directed to perform the same movements in unison. This is certainly acceptable. But the facts show that the potential physiological benefits from stretching programs are vastly overrated.

Stretching slowly and smoothly does improve a person's flexibility. Flexibility is defined as the range of movement of a body segment around a joint or group of joints. Women, because of their hormones and body composition, are generally more flexible than men. This is especially true of a woman's lower body. Yet most women seem to concentrate on movements that stretch the muscles of their hips and thighs. They mistakenly believe that stretching strengthens and firms their muscles, which it does not; that stretching lengthens their muscles, which it does not; or that stretching reduces the fatty deposits on their hips and thighs, which it does not.

Furthermore, there are no conclusive data that increased flexibility prevents injuries. Too much flexibility, in fact, can cause injuries. What research does show is that muscular strength throughout full-range joint movements is the primary factor that prevents injury.

In my opinion, you need to emphasize super-slow strength training much more than stretching movements. It is the strength of your muscles, not the flexibility of your joints, that contributes to a shapely figure.

Strength Training Without Reducing Food Calories

What about the woman who already has a low level of body fat and only needs to gain muscle?

I've worked with many women in this category. In fact, Rachelle Richardson—the woman pictured on the front cover and featured in the success story on page 23—as well as several other photographs in the book, is one of my most recent trainees. Rachelle is a high school science teacher in Gainesville, Florida. Tall and lean, she entered the program weighing 128½ pounds with her body-fat level at 13.8 percent. We were both convinced that she needed more muscle.

Rather than reduce her dietary calories, I simply recommended that she consume more carbohydrate-rich foods, begin superhydration, and strength train three times per week.

Rachelle followed the recommendations faithfully. In six weeks, her body weight increased from 128½ to 135¾ pounds. Almost all of the 7¼ pounds was muscle, muscle added to her arms, chest, back, and legs. If Rachelle continues to train seriously, she can probably add another 6 or 7 pounds of muscle to her body before she progresses to a maintenance routine. This extra muscle will almost guarantee that her figure will remain lean and defined forever.

Back and Neck Pain

Do you have any exercises for a bad back? What about a sore neck?

Four out of five women in the United States eventually suffer from lower-back pain. And neck pain is almost as prevalent. While I was director of research at Nautilus Sports/Medical Industries, we worked for many years to perfect machines that would provide safe, effective exercise for these two vulnerable areas. First, let's examine the lower back and the exercises that I recommend for it.

The primary muscles of your lower back are the erector spinae. These muscles lie on either side of your spinal column, and when they contract they extend your torso backward. The problem in designing an exercise for the lower back is one of isolation. In order for you to isolate and work only the erector spinae muscles, which is usually where the weakness lies, your pelvis must be rigidly secured. Nautilus was able to accomplish this with its machine. The concept was later improved upon by MedX Corporation, which is owned by the original founder of Nautilus.

Both Nautilus and MedX machines for the lower back can be found in fitness and sports-medicine centers. Your seat, foot position, and head stability must each be properly adjusted for the machine to function correctly, so it is important for a technician to assist you initially.

Make sure, however, that you consult with your physician before using the lower-back machine—especially if you have lower-back pain now or a history of lower-back pain.

With your physician's approval, begin with a very light resistance and apply the super-slow protocol. You should notice strength improvements in your lower-back muscles after several weeks of brief training.

The same guidelines for your lower back apply to your neck. Both Nautilus and MedX manufacture neck machines that isolate the small, often weak, muscles of your cervical spine. Once again, these machines are frequently found in fitness centers and rehabilitation clinics. Again, it's important to have a trained technician help you get situated correctly in any neck machine. Start with the lightest resistance, move slowly and smoothly, and progress gradually.

Remember, both the lower-back and neck machines should be used initially with the guidance of a trained instructor. Neither machine, however, should be added to your first six-week strength-training routine. After you master this basic routine, you may add the lower back and neck machines to your program. Doing so will lead to a stronger and healthier back and neck.

Home Exercise Machines

I frequently see commercials on television that promote various strength-training machines for use at home. Are any of them worth buying and using?

There are many machines, such as Soloflex and Nordic Flex Gold, that are highly promoted in the media. If you are looking for productive strength-training equipment at a low price, you still can't beat the old-fashioned barbell-dumbbell set. I realize, however, and so do equipment manufacturers, that no one has ever been very successful at marketing barbell-dumbbell sets for use at home. This is especially true concerning women's fitness.

As a result, most manufacturers of home strength-training equipment have pushed machines that supply resistance in the form of elastic bands or inertia reels. Elastic band machines work reasonably well only for certain short-range movements. Inertia reels supply friction-based resistance that is often termed isokinetic. The problem with isokinetic resistance is that it provides no back pressure, no eccentric contraction, and no negative resistance. Thus, you are getting only half the benefits you'd get from equipment that provides both positive and negative resistance on each repetition.

The home strength-training machines that I've seen advertised—which range in price from several hundred to several thousand dollars—usually are not well designed and do not produce efficient results. I was never able to recommend any of them.

Recently, however, I changed my mind. In early 1995 I was approached by the owners of Bowflex. They wanted me to put a small group of men and women through my six-week eating and exercise plan. But instead of using the heavy-duty equipment that I have access to at the Gainesville Health & Fitness Center, they wanted me to substitute the Bowflex system.

The Bowflex system involves an adjustable bench that is attached to a series of vertically placed power rods. The rods, which are organized in different levels of resistance, connect to cable-pulley handles. The handles adapt and adjust so that you can simulate all the popular strength-training exercises.

A bit skeptical at first, I decided to test the system with three middle-age men and three middle-age women. Six weeks later, I was pleasantly surprised. The three men had an average fat loss of 27.95 pounds and an average muscle gain of 3.7 pounds. The three women had an average fat loss of 16.96 pounds and a muscle gain of 2.73 pounds. The muscle gains were comparable to those of my previous groups who had used the equipment at the fitness center. The fat loss, however, was significantly better.

So if you're in the market for a productive, strength-training machine that you can use at home, and that sells for less than $1,000, I recommend that you check out the Bowflex system. For more information, phone (800) 654-3539.

SUCCESS STORY: NANCY YOUNG, AGE 39, HEIGHT 5'5"

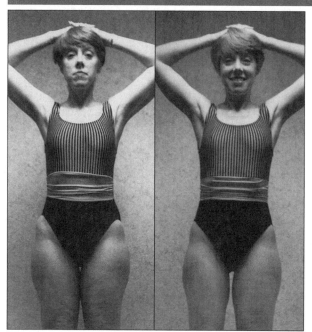

- Lost 18 pounds of fat

- Built 1¾ pounds of muscle

- Trimmed 3½ inches off her hips in 6 weeks

"Instead of using strength-training equipment at my fitness center, I applied the Bowflex routine designed by Dr. Darden. I'm so pleased with the results. I surpassed my goal of losing 15 pounds before my fortieth birthday."

Vegetarian Meals

How do you suggest that a vegetarian adapt the Body Defining *eating plan?*

Most vegetarians are very knowledgeable in the food and nutrition area. In fact, a vegetarian woman—who recently performed well on the *Body Defining* plan—revamped the menus as follows:

- Sandwich and chef salad: instead of chicken or turkey, use tofu or black beans

- Soup: instead of Healthy Choice Turkey Vegetable or Campbell's Healthy Request Hearty Chicken Rice, try Healthy Choice Garden Vegetable (220)

- Frozen microwave meals: instead of Glazed Chicken, Lasagna with Meat Sauce, and Roast Turkey, try the following: Zucchini Lasagna, Lean Cuisine (240); Marinara Twist, Lean Cuisine (240); Three Bean Chili with Rice, Lean Cuisine (210); Angel Hair Pasta, Lean Cuisine (210)

An excellent summary of the special concerns of vegetarian eating is published by the American Dietetic Association, 216 West Jackson Blvd., Suite 800, Chicago, IL 60606-6995.

Bruising

I'm halfway through the program and I'm noticing some bruising on my thighs. Why?

Black and blue marks often appear on the hips and thighs of dieting and exercising women without trauma significant enough to merit the size of the bruise. Such bruising is the result of an increased level of estrogen circulating in the body, which somehow weakens the walls of the capillaries and causes them to break under the slightest pressure. When this happens, blood escapes and a bruise occurs.

Estrogen is broken down in your liver, and so is fat. When you are losing fat, your liver preferentially breaks down the fat, leaving a lot more estrogen in your bloodstream. Supplementing your eating with 100 milligrams of vitamin C per day will help toughen the walls of the capillaries.

Cold Sensitivity

After losing more than 10 pounds, I seem to be more sensitive to cold. Why?

Some women who go through the *Body Defining* course do complain about being cold much of the time. Even during the summer, air-conditioning can bring on the chills. So can drinking the recommended amounts of cold water each day.

Much of your fat is located right under your skin and acts as insulation. Once you begin to lose this insulation, it's no wonder that you become more sensitive to cold. Your fingers, toes, and even the tip of your nose can be affected.

Before you put on a sweater or coat, remember that the state of almost shivering is one of the best ways to burn calories. Move around, take a walk, and try to keep the sweater off a little longer. Train your body to generate its own heat. You'll burn more fat in the process.

100 Days to Overlearning

How can I keep fat off permanently?

The key to permanent fat loss is overlearning. Overlearning requires the practice of the salient guidelines—eat smaller meals more frequently, emphasize carbohydrate-rich foods, apply superhydration, and strength train three times per week—until they are internalized.

The women who have gone through my programs, lost significant amounts of fat, and kept it off are the ones who have internalized the guidelines. How long does it take to overlearn and internalize?

As a general rule, behavioral psychologists say it takes 21 days to establish a pattern and 100 days to make it automatic.

I've noticed similar time spans among my participants. The *Body Defining* program gets easier for most women after three weeks. If they continue with the plan for three months, their daily actions become almost automatic. Be aware, too, that many psychologists believe that the 100-day time span means 100 consecutive days. If you practice the discipline for 90 days and break the pattern on day 91, then you must start over. Maybe that's why it's so hard for most people to keep the fat off.

It's certainly possible for some people to do. I've seen many succeed. In spite of family responsibilities, divorce, lack of money, serious accidents, job relocations, and deaths of friends, they have not regained their lost fat. What started out as guidelines have become habits. The habits then become internalized and are overlearned; they persist even when stressful events occur.

Overlearning is the key. Make 100 consecutive days your goal.

Eliminate, or Accentuate, Strength Training?

Can I go through the Body Defining *eating plan without doing the strength-training program?*

No. You'd be making the same mistake that many women who have been unsuccessful at losing fat and keeping it off have made before you. I want you to lose the fat and keep it off finally and forever.

Without strength training, a significant amount of your weight loss will come from your muscles. As I've stated throughout this book, building your muscles is a major factor in permanent fat loss. Your muscles are the central factor in physical fitness and the key for this entire book.

Muscle-building exercise requires the use of progressively heavier weights, or overload—and overloading your body correctly is not fun. It involves a great deal of effort on your part.

Exercise must be demanding to be meaningful. Don't let anyone convince you that there is value in what is called effortless exercise. Effortless exercise makes about as much sense as a foodless meal.

Decide today that you can adapt your body to both the *Body Defining* eating plan and the *Body Defining* strength-training program. Your overall results will be impressive and enduring.

Chapter 20

Well Defined Forever!

If you follow the guidelines in this book, there's no reason why you can't have a defined body for life. You're going to know how to eat and how to exercise properly under almost any circumstance.

You're going to be stronger and leaner, with greater endurance.

You're going to look terrific. With your new figure, you're going to have fun shopping for clothes—even swimsuits and evening dresses—and you'll wear them with pride.

Losing fat, building muscle, and getting defined will free you from the confinement of your own self-consciousness so that you can be more caring and more giving to others.

You'll be eager to accept new challenges, to meet different people, and to participate in activities you may never have considered before.

And you'll be transforming your way to confidence and happiness.

Enjoy your well-defined body now and forever!

About the Author

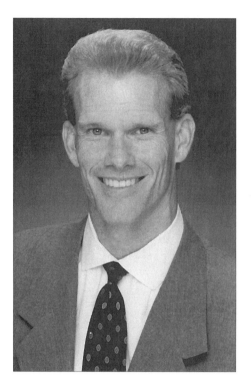

Ellington Darden, Ph.D., is the founding director of research for Nautilus Sports/Medical Industries, author of 43 books on physical fitness, and a leading expert on strength training.

Through his programs and courses, he transforms the weak and the fat into the strong and the lean. With his unwavering support and a moderate amount of self-discipline, participants can metamorphosize their bodies into better shape than they've ever imagined. This in turn takes them many steps down the road to life-long health and vitality.

Dr. Darden's outstanding research was recognized in 1989 when he was honored as one of the top ten health leaders in the United States by the President's Council on Physical Fitness and Sports.

He received his bachelor's and master's degrees in physical education from Baylor University. He studied five years at Florida State University, where he earned his doctorate in exercise science and completed two years of postdoctorate work in food and nutrition.

As a man tirelessly dedicated to improving the physical well-being of his clients, Dr. Darden reveals one regret: "I wish I could change more lives, especially women in this country. There's such an abundance of fitness misinformation in the United States, and it seems to escalate each day. Sometimes I feel I need to stand in the middle of every supermarket, stop each woman, and share with her how important it is for her to keep her muscles strong. Somehow, some way I've got to make my voice heard above all the riffraff. It's my personal goal to accomplish this in my lifetime."

Ellington Darden frequently talks at conventions and seminars throughout the United States. For a listing of his speaking engagements, please send a self-addressed, stamped envelope to Living Longer Stronger, 10 N. Meade Ave., Colorado Springs, CO 80909, or phone (719) 473-7000.

*Stay in control
of your
strength, sharpness,
and
symmetry!*